Stuka
at
War

Stuka at War

Peter C. Smith

LONDON
IAN ALLAN LTD

By the same author:—
Destroyer Leader
Task Force 57
Pedestal
Hard Lying
British Battle Cruisers
Heritage of the Sea
Royal Navy Ships Badges
Battles of the Malta Striking Forces (With Edwin Walker)
R.A.F. Squadron Badges
The Story of the Torpedo Bomber
War in the Aegean (With Edwin Walker)
Per Mare Per Terram
Arctic Victory
Fighting Flotilla
The Battle of Midway
The Great Ships Pass
Hit First, Hit Hard
Action Imminent

Anthologies (as Editor and Contributor)
Destroyer Action
The Haunted Sea
Undesirable Properties
The Phantom Coach
Haunted Shores

First published 1971
This edition 1980

ISBN 0 7110 1017 X

Published by Ian Allan Ltd, Shepperton, Surrey, and printed by Ian Allan Printing Ltd at their works at Coombelands in Runnymede, England

Contents

	Foreword	5
	Introduction	6
1	Early Developments	8
2	The First Tests	21
3	Race to the Sea	33
4	Closing the Channel	49
5	Début in the Mediterranean	57
6	The Killing Ground	66
7	Training, Techniques and Tactics	78
8	Smashing the Soviets	85
9	Bane of the Convoys	95
10	The Carrier that Never Was	105
11	The Defences Harden	110
12	Duel in the Darkness	120
	Appendices	128

Foreword

I was very happy to be asked to read through and contribute a Foreword to Peter Smith's *Stuka at War*. When I first joined the Air Force, I had wanted to be a fighter pilot, but I soon became proud to fly the Stuka. Although I understand this aircraft has earned an undeserved reputation in the west, to me the Stuka was a joy to fly. Not only was it a good plane in the air, but it was also reliable and strong, and I owed my life on many occasions to the sturdiness of this little bomber.

As the war progressed several new aircraft were designed and built to be in all respects superior to the Junkers Ju87, but somehow none of these ever really replaced the Stuka in combat and most veteran pilots preferred to stay with it. I always knew that I could depend on my Stuka to get me home and only once did it fail me.

I wish this interesting book the success it most surely deserves.

Hans-Ulrich Rudel
Kufstein, Tyrol
August 1970

Introduction

This is the story of one of the most famous aircraft of World War II, the Junkers Ju87 dive-bomber, and also of the part this inverted gull-winged aircraft played in the Luftwaffe's challenge to Britain's control of the coastal sea. No aircraft gained greater notoriety nor commanded greater respect from its opponents than the Stuka* in the opening months of the war. Because of this, and because of the numerous successes it

*Stuka is, of course, a contraction of the German word *Sturzkampfflugzeug*, meaning all dive-bombers, but throughout the war and since the name has come to represent the Ju87.

achieved in both defeating armies and disputing control of the sea, I felt that the Stuka story was worth recording. Many people have warned me that the Ju87 was regarded as a failure in Britain. Nevertheless it is a fact that this angular machine did more than any other weapon in Germany's armoury to make possible their most spectacular victories.

This book is much concerned with the maritime use of the Stuka, as well as the land battles, and it was one of the greatest ironies of all that much of the potential of the dive-bomber as a ship-busting weapon was demon-

strated to the Germans very early in the war by the British themselves, by the Royal Navy in fact. The sinking of the German light cruiser *Königsberg* at Bergen on 10 April 1940 by 15 Skua dive-bombers of the Fleet Air Arm gave proof of the superiority of this method of aerial attack over the high-level methods which had up until then failed so obviously when mounted by Wellington or Heinkel.

The British appeared blind to their success and soon afterwards the Skua squadrons were disbanded, but Germany, with the most powerful dive-bomber force in the world, took note. The *Königsberg* was to be avenged many times over in the years that followed.

This book does not pretend to be the complete and final word of the Stuka story, but it is hoped that the story as here related and the selection of photographs, will appeal to all aviation enthusiasts.

I should like to express my thanks to Alfred Price, Franz Selinger, Gary Owens, Christyl Styles, Willie Radinger, 'Archie' Rowlands and Hanfried Schliephake for the assistance they have given me in the creation of this book and for the encouragement they offered me. I should also like to thank the staff of the Imperial War Museum Photo and Film sections for the assistance they have given me so freely, and Ullstein of Berlin. Special thanks of course to Hans-Ulrich Rudel and many others, in Germany and Britain.

Introduction to the Revised Edition

I would like to add thanks to those who contributed their own views, stories and eye-witness accounts for this new edition of my book. Maj Friedrich Lang; Generalleutnant a.D Helmut Mahlke; Ing Hans Drescher; Maj Waldemar Plewig. Thanks also to Günthe Behling of Traditionsgemeinschaft des Stuka-geschwaders 2 'Immelmann', to Nicola Malizia for information on Italian Stuka units and to Helga Hinsby for the invaluable translation work she performed for me.

It is hoped that the inclusion of this fresh eyewitness documentation will bring a new dimension to my book and afford a chance to see things 'from the other side of the hill' as it were, on what flying the Stuka was like.

Peter C. Smith
Needingworth, Cambs

June 1979

1 Early Developments

The Ju87 dive-bomber achieved almost legendary fame during the opening years of World War II. With its evil, inverted gull-wing shape, its frightful and unearthly howl as it attacked and, above all, its deadly accuracy as it pin-pointed and destroyed vital targets like gun batteries, bridges, ammunition dumps and power stations, the Stuka became the most feared weapon in the sky. Strangely enough, despite its early triumphs in the field of combat, the German Air Staff had been largely divided as to its usefulness before the war, and only when it had proven itself during the speedy campaigns which defeated Poland and France, did the German propaganda machine start to boast of the 'Supreme Weapon'.

Vertical bombing had been tried, with varying degrees of success, during World War I, and continued tests with specially adapted biplanes in the 1920s had shown that the percentage of hits on a select target became much greater by using this technique than with the more normal horizontal method. It must be remembered that bomb-sights were primitive at this time and would remain so until well into the 1940s.

Early German experiments had been conducted with the Ju87's legitimate predecessor, the Junkers K47. This machine was the brainchild of Karl Plauth, the former leader of Jasta 51 with 17 'kills' to his credit, and he had originally intended his design to be a two-seater fighter. All production of military aircraft in Germany was banned under the terms of the Versailles Treaty, but when the K47 first appeared in 1927 it was as a civilian sports plane under the designation Junkers A48. Actually the ban was easily evaded, for, under the able guidance of Gen von Seeckt, the nucleus of a future military air arm had already been formed in the Weimar Republic as early as 1920, and selected officers were sent to the aviation ministry from where they organised a reserve of trained aviators.

Below: The Junkers K47 – the Stuka's grandfather. */Archiv Schliephake*

Top right: Bomb racks fitted to the K47, which was a fighter design that gave birth to the dive-bomber concept again in Germany. */Archiv Schliephake*

Centre right: Bomb in stowed position on the K47 for trials. */Archiv Schliephake*

Below right: Designer Pohlmann with Junkers' workers./*Archiv Schliephake*

Below far right: Wolfram Freiherr von Richthofen, related to the famous ace of World War I, he was initially totally against the dive-bomber concept, but in Spain and Poland he was instrumental in perfecting the close-support technique in which they played such a leading part./*Ullstein*

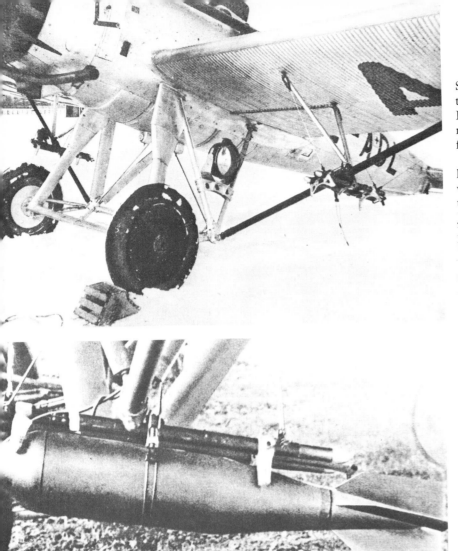

Further, a secret agreement with the Soviet Union saw the establishment of a testing centre for both pilots and machines at Lipetz, and through this school passed the majority of the front-line crewmen of the future Luftwaffe and its leaders.

Plauth therefore had no trouble in having his machine evaluated and intensive tests were carried out resulting in the building of three military variations of the K48 at the Junkers Swedish aircraft factory at Limnham. Plauth himself was killed in an air accident before his initial design had been proven, but the K48 was put through its paces at Lipetz and showed itself to be a rugged machine and a stable bombing platform.

Among the tests was one which featured bomb-racks fitted to the machine on sloping struts, and the aircraft was found to perform well in simulated dive-bombing rôles. Swedish Junkers felt encouraged enough to proceed with further designs as private ventures. A design team was set up under Pohlmann and the first prototypes were built during 1934–35.

By this time, however, the Nazi party led by Adolf Hitler had come to power and Goering appointed Wolfram von Richthofen as the new head of the Technical Office at the Air Ministry. Richthofen was absolutely against dive-bombing concepts for he felt that for any aircraft to dive below 6,000ft in the face of anti-aircraft fire would be suicidal, and that the slow, low-flying aircraft of this type would be annihilated in wartime. He therefore stopped all developments on these lines.

9

Meanwhile, in the United States, the Navy had continued to develop the dive-bombing technique for their carrier-based attack squadrons, the Helldivers, and, using Curtiss Hawk biplanes, they put on many flying displays across the country. It was here that fate played a hand, for it was now that Ernst Udet, later to be known as the originator of the Stuka, while on tour in the States, first became impressed at the potential of these aircraft during 1931.

Two years later, when Goering in the capacity of Reich Commissioner of Aviation was busy recruiting ex-World War I fliers to fill posts in the new Luftwaffe, he contacted Udet. Udet, ranking as among the most famous surviving aces in Germany, was an obvious choice but his happy-go-lucky nature baulked at the prospect of losing his independence as a stunt pilot. Goering, however, was aware of his fascination with the Hawks and through his ministry bought two for evaluation at the Tempelhof airfield test centre.

The results of these tests were not satisfactory to the assembled watchers, which included Milch and Kesselring, but far from dissuading Udet, they resulted in repeated tests of his own which only confirmed in his mind the need for such a bomber in the Luftwaffe. Finally, rather than give up his idea, he agreed to join the Luftwaffe himself and in January 1936 he was made Inspector of Fighters. It was still the dive-bomber concept which held his fascination, however, and unofficially he encouraged the firms with such projects on hand to continue their

Above: Ernst Udet – World War I ace, interwar stunt pilot, erstwhile playboy. His obsession with dive-bombing was a factor in the spread of the doctrine in the prewar Luftwaffe. /*Ullstein*

Left: Junkers Ju87V1, the first prototype with twin tailplanes. /*Archiv Schliephake*

Top right: Junkers Ju87V2, second prototype with modified tail./*Archiv Schliephake*

Centre right: Close-up of the Ju87V2 with the Rolls-Royce Kestrel V engine. /*Franz Selinger*

Right: An aerial view of the Ju87V3, third prototype. /*Archiv Schliephake*

research, in flat contradiction to the official line as laid down by Richthofen.

Pohlmann's Junkers team had been doing just that and by the end of 1935 the Ju87v1 had been completed and evaluated. This aircraft featured the unique inverted gull configuration and a twin tail assembly like its predecessor the K42. Power was provided by a single Rolls-Royce Kestrel V water-cooled 12-cylinder engine driving a fixed-pitch two-blade wooden airscrew. The fixed undercarriage was of the trouser-type fixed gear favoured by the sports machines of that period.

The bomb load was slung under the wings and fuselage and defensive armament comprised a single rear-firing movable M15 gun and two forward firing M15s in the body firing over the engine. Flight testing of this machine resulted in the replacement of the Kestrel engine by a 610hp 12-cylinder liquid-cooled engine with a metal airscrew. The tail unit emerged on the new model, the Ju87v, as a single fin and rudder assembly.

The Ju87v underwent evaluation at the Luftwaffe Research Establishment at Rechlin, where, during the autumn of 1935, while undergoing a diving test, it shed its tail unit and plunged into the ground. To prevent this happening again, as the angle of the dive was increasing under tests, special dive-brakes were designed by Junkers. These took the form of slats mounted abaft the leading edges of the wings, outboard of the main undercarriage members. These brakes were designed to bring the speed of the diving aircraft to under 375mph which Pohlmann's team felt

was the limit a machine could stand without breaking up.

Successfully tested, they were incorporated in the Ju87v3, which also had stability modifications to the tail unit and a redesigned engine cowling which afforded the pilot a better view.

Current bombing tests with horizontal bombers had not achieved the percentage of hits considered satisfactory and the advocates of dive-bombing were pressing the RLM (Technical Office) with their ideas. An added attraction to Goering was the point they made which stated that the accuracy of the technique would enable a single dive-bomber to knock out a pinpoint target as against a whole squadron of horizontal bombers using the area bombing method. Being charged with building up the German air force to a high enough potential to back up Hitler's Grand Strategy for Europe after a 15-year standstill, was proving a more exacting task than he had imagined and this idea of cost effectiveness was very attractive.

Trials were held at Rechlin by the RLM to determine which of four current machines should be adopted as the German Air Force's standard dive-bomber. Junkers, with their early lead, were in a strong position from the outset. Against the Ju87v2 were pitted the Ha137, a single-engined monoplane, and the Arado Ar81, a two-seat biplane. Both of these were eliminated early in the contest, but Junkers' closest competitor was the Heinkel He118, which was also equipped with the

12

Kestrel engine. This aircraft was a trim, pleasing aircraft and proved to be faster than the Ju87V2, but it was not selected. The tests ended with little to choose between the two machines although the Junkers product appeared to be more favoured.

A major point against the He118 was that Udet, in a further flight to satisfy himself, crashed when the aircraft shed its airscrew. Probably the deciding factor in the final selection was the sturdiness of the Junkers and its adaptability for mass production, both very important points in 1936.

The final prototype was the Ju87V4 which featured the new dive-bombing release fork. This device was mounted under the body and held the 550lb bomb in a cradle which, when released, swung the missile out and down to clear the aircraft propeller arc. Also at this time, Junkers brought out the auto-pilot developed by Askania. This was found to be necessary because it was common to find that the pressure to which the Stuka pilot was subjected to on pulling out of his power dive, often made him black out and lose control. Tested by female test pilot Melitta Schiller, this device was first fitted to the 10 pre-production models, designated the Ju87A0.

Richthofen, adamant as ever, ordered the cessation of all further work on the Ju87, but on 10 June he was undermined by the appointment of Udet himself to the command of the Technical Office where he could now press his idea and adopted brainchild to the limit. Meanwhile, the Civil War in Spain was under way and in response to appeals to Hitler from Franco a number of Luftwaffe personnel and aircraft were sent there to render assistance. The Legion Kondor was formed and Richthofen was despatched as its Chief of Staff.

During raids on Madrid and other towns during 1936–37, the basic fighter component of the Legion Kondor, the He51, had been proven too slow and vulnerable against the latest American and Russian types used by the defence and at the beginning of 1937 had to be withdrawn. In March of that year three Staffeln of these fighters were fitted with racks to carry ten 10kg bombs for ground-attack and these were followed by the Ha123. The success of these units led to the birth of the Schlachtflieger (Ground Attack Units), and much of the credit rested with Richthofen himself, who developed this form of attack to a fine art. By the end of the year the first three Ju87s had arrived on the scene. These were Ju87A1s.

This aircraft was basically a Ju87V4 with simplified wing form to speed mass production and three of these were sent for evaluation tests under war conditions in December. These were of the A1 variant and were powered by the Junkers Jumo 210Da engine of 635hp. The first unit to be equipped with this plane was the Immelmann Sturzkampfgeschwader and this unit took part in the occupation of Czechoslovakia. By September 1938 the Ju87 was equipping four Gruppen. The Stuka itself was regarded chiefly as a weapon for

Top left: Junkers Ju87V4. Prototype of the A series. /*Archiv Schliephake*

Centre left: A Junkers Ju87A1 (D-IEAU) of 1/StG162. /*Franz Selinger*

Below left: A Junkers Ju87A1 in 1937 'splinter' markings. /*Archiv Schliephake*

Below: A Ju87A1 with early markings, note the huge wheel 'trousers'. /*Bundesarchiv*

back area bombing (Nahkampfkorps), and its introduction in strength amounted to a reverse suffered by the supporters of real close-support.

The Ju87A1 had a performance of poor quality. A maximum speed of 199mph at 12,000ft, unladen, with a maximum range of 620 miles. Normal bomb load was a single 550lb bomb, but they could be adapted to carry a single 1,100lb bomb by the expedient of dropping one crew member. Initial tests over Spain proved that the A1 was underpowered, and Pohlmann and his team developed the Ju87B0 which utilised the Jumo 211D engine, had a redesigned cockpit canopy and maximum speed was thereby increased to 234mph at 15,000ft and the bomb load went up to one 1,100lb or one 550lb and four 110lb bombs with full crew. Range increased to 370 miles, fully laden.

The armament was also improved with the rear-firing gun retained but with two MG17 guns mounted in the wings. Landing speed was 67·1mph. An altitude of 3,280ft could be obtained in 120 seconds. The trouser casing on the wheels gave way to streamlined spats. Weight loaded was 7,495lb and unladen 5,104lb and dimensions were: span 45ft, length 35ft 5in, height 12ft 9in approx. The Ju87B was to form the bulk of the Stuka units on the Luftwaffe strength in September 1939.

Only three Ju87A1s were initially sent to Spain but a continuous turn-round of crews ensured that the maximum number of pilots acquainted themselves with combat conditions. Always a rather ungainly aircraft, the first group to join the Legion Kondor were dubbed Jolanthe after a pig which featured in a stage comedy success in Germany at that time, Krach um Jolanthe (Trouble about

Jolanthe), and the unit adopted the pig symbol as their special marking on the port wheel spat.

The Stukas were employed in most theatres of the Spanish Civil War, at Teruel initially and then on the Ebro front and Catalonia. With the new Messerschmitt Bf109 proving its absolute superiority over anything the Russians could supply to the Republican forces, the Stuka pilots had no worries about enemy interceptors and the only opposition they generally had to endure was flak of the more primitive kind.

The morale of troops when subjected to dive-bombing was found to be very low and to increase this effect Udet had the idea of increasing the natural howling of the power dive by the addition of a siren on the leg of the landing gear. This simple device had an effect quite out of proportion to its value – and not only in Spain. Combined with the roaring engines and the thud of exploding bombs, and added to the fact that a dive-bomber in a power-dive always appears to be aiming specifically at you, many troops broke and fled in the French and British armies. The Luftwaffe pilots christened it the Trombone of Jericho and its effect was yet another factor in the Stuka legend, although after 1941 its use was discontinued.

It was during this campaign that the tentative idea of using the Stukas as a mobile artillery barrage began to crystallise, and indeed the Ju87 was one of the outstanding successes of the Legion Kondor intervention. Swiftly following the ebb and flow of the land battle and always appearing at the crucial moment in their screaming dives, their skill in placing a bomb on a target with an accuracy of under 30yd was impressive.

The Stuka was popular with its crew also, for despite the alarming tales spread by Allied sources during the war in an attempt to debunk its merits, it was an extremely agile machine. One RAF pilot, G. R. S. McKay, who actually flew a captured Ju87 on many occasions has recently described its flying characteristics as

Top left: A Ju87A1 in Spanish markings with the Legion Kondor – note the 'Jolanthe' insignia on the wheel trouser. |*Franz Selinger*

Centre left: A Junkers Ju87A1 with Spanish Nationalist markings, serving with the 'Jolanthe Kette'. |*Archiv Schliephake*

Below left: Across the dusty airstrip in Spain the Kette of StG163 scrambles away. |*Archiv Schliephake*

Right: The Junkers Ju87BO. |*Radinger*

Below: A nice clear prewar shot of a Ju87B1 in early markings on a grass strip.|*IWM*

Above left: Somewhat primitive by today's standards, the Dessau production line in the 1930s./*Archiv Schliephake*

Above: The Stuka production line at Junkers' Dessau works./*Archiv Schliephake*

Left: Production in full swing at Dessau – lowering the engine into position.
/*Archiv Schliephake*

Below: Engine assembly and fitting at Dessau.
/*Archiv Schliephake*

Above right: Final touches on the line.
/*Archiv Schliephake*

Above far right: Stukas nearing completion at Dessau./*Archiv Schliephake*

Right: Last check before the first flight of a production line Stuka./*Archiv Schliephake*

Below right: A completed batch of Ju87B8s awaiting delivery to their units.
/*Archiv Schliephake*

16

excellent, the controls as being so light that there was a marked tendency to over-control. Visibility was excellent and the cockpit very roomy. The controls were simple to handle and he found the plane wholly suggested power and strength.

Full-scale production of the Ju87B was switched to the Weser Flugzeugbau works at Tempelhof, a subsidiary of the Deschimag section of Krupp-Werks, who remained responsible for all further developments and production of the Stuka.

Thus with the competition of the Spanish Civil War the returning Luftwaffe pilots were completely acquainted and indeed heavily influenced by the effect of the dive-bomber, and in fact all the bomber units had achieved impressive results with close-support action in conjunction with ground forces. Von Richthofen had shown how a tactical air force could paralyse opposing armies by concentration at the vital points and he was to demonstrate his tactic only too well in the years ahead.

Experience with the effects of dive-bombing against shipping also proceeded satisfactorily and the final operations in Spain saw the Stuka employed in this rôle against ships and docks on the Mediterranean coast where lay the final Republican strongholds. *Junkers Nachrichten*, the company house journal, wrote in the June 1939 edition that: 'The havoc wrought in the port areas of Valencia, Tarragona, Barcelona, etc is chiefly due to the activities of the dive-bombers, which also accounted for a large proportion of the ships wrecked or sunk.'

However, anti-shipping strikes did not figure at all in the thoughts of the Luftwaffe High Command as they considered the implications of the Führer's determination to smash Poland over the Danzig issue. Close support for the Army by all air arms was the lesson that was initially digested. Although Maj Harlinghausen had been transferred

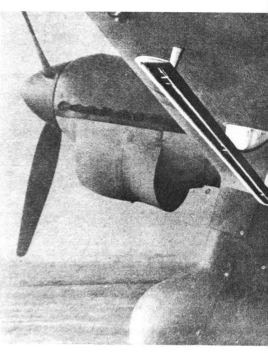

18

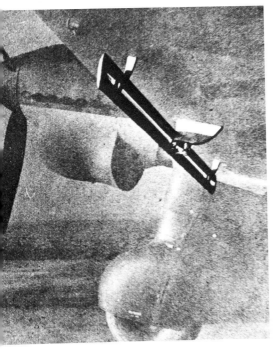

Above far left: B1s replaced the A series in the Legion Kondor and they also adopted 'Jolanthe'. /*Archiv Schliephake*

Above left, above: Detail of Stuka dive brake workings. /*Archiv Schliephake*

Above right: Instrument layout in the cockpit of a Ju87B1. /*Archiv Schliephake*

Left: A Kette of Ju87Bs also later went to work in Spain. /*Archiv Schliephake*

Right: Oberst Walter Sigel. He led the doomed 1/StG76 when it made its fatal dive at Neuhammer in August 1939, but escaped death./*Ullstein*

secretly to the embryo Air Force in 1933 to initiate maritime air operations, and had led a bomber unit in Spain, he was unable to convince the High Command of the importance of this branch. They had been assured by Hitler that war against England and her Navy would not come until 1944 and they made their plans accordingly.

The German Air Staff regarded the dive-bomber as the major instrument for destroying vital objectives in the heart of enemy industrial centres as well as tactical objectives such as bridges, ammunition, fuel and food dumps, and the recent example of Spain had shown its power to affect morale. In these rôles it was to prove completely effective as long as air opposition had been eliminated, but it was not the close-support theory as advocated by Richthofen.

By no means all the German officers were convinced of the Stuka's rôle, but with nine dive-bomber Geschwader, with a total establishment strength of 336 Ju87As and Bs in August 1939, it was clear that the dive-bomber was committed to playing a major rôle in the forthcoming offensive. Before the war actually broke out the supporters of the Stuka received one extremely unpleasant shock.

Preparatory to moving up to its attack positions against Poland 1/StG76, under the command of Hauptmann Sigel, had been briefed to lay on a demonstration of precision dive-bombing with smoke bombs, at the training ground at Neuhammer. Watching would be Generalleutnant von Richthofen, who, although still retaining his misgivings about the Stuka, was to lead them into action that same month. Also present were Hugo von Sperrle and Bruno Loerzer. The weather report was 7/10 cloud cover over the target from

Above: Ju87 'Antons' in January, 1938, serving with III/StG163 in Langensalza. /*Waldemar Plewig*

Right: During the bloodless occupation of Czechoslovakia in 1938 several Stuka units moved into the occupied areas. Here the German pilots relax with Slovakian army officers. /*Waldemar Plewig*

2,500 to 6,000ft but good visibility below that level and Sigel made his dispositions accordingly. His three Staffeln, comprising 30 aircraft in all, were organised in three groups in wedge-shaped formation. They were instructed to approach the target from 12,000ft, dive through the cloud layer and release their bombs at 1,000ft.

Unfortunately in the hour between the weather reconnaissance report and the arrival of 1/StG76 over the target a thick ground mist developed, information of which had not been passed on to the airborne Gruppe. Consequently they commenced their dives as normal. Sigel himself realised what had occurred at the last second and pulled up with a bare 6ft to spare, shouting a desperate warning to his companions as he did so. It was too late to save most of them and with a scream of sirens they plunged one after another at high speed hard into the ground.

A few managed to pull up like their leader, but several of these became entangled in the trees of the surrounding forest and were also wiped out. In all, 13 Stukas were lost in as many seconds with their entire crews. It had been a ghastly accident. A subsequent enquiry cleared Sigel, who went on to become one of the ace Stuka pilots of the war, and it had no effect on the operational use of the aircraft, but opponents of the Ju87 have since seized on the incident to demonstrate the aircraft's unwieldy handling characteristics.

This proved nothing of the sort, it was certainly not the cause of the accident, and indeed but for the manoeuvrability of the Stuka not 13 but 30 aircraft would have been lost that day. There was little the dispirited Udet could do other than mourn the loss of 26 of his finest aircrew, for two weeks later the Stuka units were spearheading the initial thrusts of World War II as the Wehrmacht crossed the Polish border on 1 September 1939.

2 The First Tests

The Stuka can claim the dubious distinction of being the first aircraft to carry out a bombing mission in World War II. At Dirschau, on the Vistula, were twin bridges carrying vital rail links, and to facilitate the rapid link-up between the German Army Groups coming west from Germany and south-east from East Prussia, it was essential that the Poles were prevented from destroying them.

An armoured train was prepared to seize and hold the bridges, but long before it could hope to arrive specially prepared detonation charges would have torn the bridges asunder. It was therefore entrusted to a Kette, from 3/StG1 led by Bruno Dilley, to knock out the detonation points in a surprise raid destined to take place 15min before the German troops erupted over the border from their start lines.

It was a difficult mission, for although the exact location of the target had been pin-pointed, they were merely small areas on a map. It would require the greatest precision to hit them and for several days pilots from 3/StG1 had been training at Insteburg airfield to strike them first time. The preparations had been planned in the greatest detail and several of the bomber crews had ridden the train route over the bridge to gain eye-witness detail of the surrounding area. It was decided to go in at very low level to reduce human error to the minimum.

Bad weather conditions prevailed all along the front on the 1st which severely hampered the Luftwaffe's initial efforts and the Polish Air Force was not, as has been so often stated, destroyed on the ground. Dilley's Kette, although based a mere eight minutes' flight from its target, had a terrible time. They took off at 0426hrs and hedge-hopped through the fog and mist towards the target, but on making contact with the Vistula river, they turned north and followed it up to the bridges. At 0435 all three Stukas flying at 30ft released their bombs plumb on target and swooped away. Despite their accuracy and the fact that the Stukas succeeded in severing the leads to the detonators, the Poles managed to carry out repairs and thus destroy the bridge, although one still stood when the armoured train finally arrived on the scene.

Here, right at the beginning of the war, was demonstrated the Stuka's greatest asset – accuracy; by comparison the high-level raids which followed merely destroyed a large part of the town.

Giving the world the first demonstration

Below: Two mechanics engaged in primitive refuelling operations on a home airfield. */IWM*

of the Blitzkreig technique, the Luftwaffe had concentrated the bulk of its forces against Poland, hoping thus to afford a quick decision before the French could attack in the rear. Later they realised that they had nothing to fear in the way of such aggressiveness from the Western Allies, but at the time the threat was a real one and it says much for the boldness of the German High Command that the risk was accepted.

In all, 219 Ju87B dive-bombers were available to the great air fleets. Luftflotte 1, commanded by Kesselring, had II and III/StG2 and IV(Stuka)/LG1 under its command, and Luftflotte 4, under Löhr, had StG77 and (St)LG2, led by Richthofen.

Because of the weather it was afternoon before the full weight of these forces were directed against the Polish defences but when they finally got airborne, the Stukas soon pulverised the dazed Poles.

Dilley was airborne for the second time that fateful day when I/StG1 bombed the radio stations of Warsaw at Babice and Lacy, but such targets as radio masts were hard to destroy as the explosions had little effect other than to make them rock with the blast, and the attack was not a complete success. It was to prove a forerunner of the frustration they were to undergo when instructed to destroy Britain's radar network.

Waldemar Plewig had transferred to the Luftwaffe in 1935 after serving as a Leutnant in Infantry Regiment 7. In 1937 he became Staffelführer of III/StG162 (afterwards I/StG163) and then moved on to II/StG162 (afterwards I/StG163) based at Langensalza, which was renamed III/StG2 'Immelmann' in 1939, being promoted to Hauptmann on 1

January of that year. He describes that unit's movements during the Polish campaign as follows:

'From our home base of Langensalza we moved up to Stolp, and from here we carried out the operations against the Polish fleet at Hela; then we moved to advance airfields near Olmutz and after that to Michalowze (Slovakia). From all these fields we flew numerous operations against warships and Polish aerodromes and in support of the army.

'The first mission was marked by the aerial fight between Leutnant Goring's Ju87 and a Polish fighter, which resulted in our first loss, and this made the most impression on me. On my own return flight from this sortie, I flew at low level and over the Tucherler Heath came under small-arms fire, which riddled my machine with bullets. It was a surprise to me at just how much punishment of this sort my Ju87 could take and still get me home.

'We were briefed before the sortie that should we have to crash land because of damage, we were not just to destroy our machine, but to take our own lives as well, because the partisans would show us no mercy! One of my men returned to the squadron after a very long and terrible endurance march through enemy-occupied territory.

'In Slovakia when we set up our advanced bases the Slovakian army was of the utmost help and we worked together well in the air as well, for on our army support missions we usually flew with Slovakian fighter cover. Our success rate was high on assigned targets, although naturally there were some missions when things went wrong, for example our bombs would fall between the rails and still

Above left: Haupt Bruno Dilley. He led the first bombing attack of World War II in a Stuka. /*Ullstein*

Above: The Polish campaign initiated the devastating combination of Stuka and Panzer in 1939. /*Archiv Schliephake*

Above right: Beginning of the war, II/StG77 awaiting sortie orders against Polish targets. /*Waldemar Plewig*

Centre right: Typical Stuka targets, the railway station and vital marshalling yards are hit during the Polish Campaign. /*Waldemar Plewig*

Bottom right: A personal touch! A special message for the Poles. /*Waldemar Plewig*

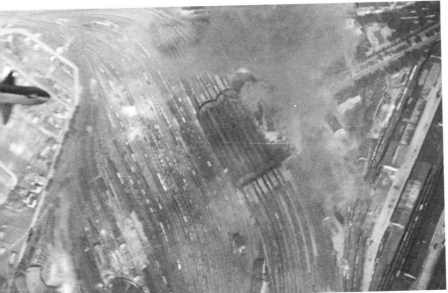

not blow up the bridge target, but our losses were light. After the Polish campaign, while the unit was in transit back to its home base, one of my transport Ju52s got caught in a balloon cable near Weimer, but that was one of my few losses. After various moves that winter after we got home early in 1940 we arrived at Cologne. Here my unit, II/StG77, of which I was Staffelkapitän, rested and trained for the operations in the west and I was promoted to Gruppe Kommandant in April, 1940.'

II and III/StG2 cooperated with IV(Stuka)/LG1 and the Naval dive-bomber squadron, 4/186, in attacks on Polish naval units and harbour installations. In all, 120 Ju87s were sent against Poland's tiny navy, backed up by sorties by six of Germany's big modern destroyers. The German Navy had the humiliation of being driven off by the spirited resistance of the Polish warships but, swamped by dive-bombers, they lost the destroyer *Mazur* at Okrywie. She was hit several times and sank immediately after an attack by IV(Stuka)/LG1 led by Hauptmann Kögl.

Widespread devastation was caused and after the first day under Stuka attack the Polish Navy almost ceased to exist. The submarines *Rys* and *Sep* were damaged, and the gunboat *General Haller* was sunk on 6 September. Other victims of the first mass Stuka assault against warships were the minesweepers *Czapla*, *Jaskolka*, *Mewa*, and several auxiliaries. Many of the larger vessels, although attacked and hit and damaged, managed to escape to Britain, but others were trapped and sought refuge in Puck Bay.

Further strikes were made and the survivors fled to Hela. It was planned to finish them off by naval assault and the bulk of the Stuka forces under Grauert were switched to ground targets. In this field Richthofen's units were already blooded.

Under the command of Oskar Dinort, I/StG2 had managed to make attacks on airfields at Cracow while other Stuka strikes went in against Katowitz and Wadowice, but despite hits on hangars and installations they found that the birds had flown. Most of the Polish fighter force had managed to get airborne and they fought bravely, but their machines were completely outclassed and they were unable even to catch modern bombers like the Dornier Do17 and the Heinkel He111. Outclassed and outnumbered they were soon wiped out.

Likewise the Polish Army was mainly equipped with obsolete equipment and outdated ideas. Being the first nation to be on the receiving end of the new German method of massed tanks, mobile infantry and continuous air support, it is not surprising that they found their armies encircled and forced back all along the front. Even so, the Polish Army put up a much more spirited resistance than the Western Allies the following spring, and they caused far greater casualties to the German Army.

The Ju87 was on call everywhere to smash defences and break up resistance before it became organised. I/StG76, re-equipped after its ordeal in August and still led by Sigel, put in a precision attack on defence works at Wielun and I/StG77 commanded by Oberst Schwarzkopff, known as the 'Stuka Father', wiped out Polish positions at Lublinitz.

It was a one-sided contest for the Stuka pilots in many cases. After the morning attacks on airfields I/StG2, flying from Nieder-Ellguth base, found and attacked a whole Polish Cavalry Brigade it found assembling in the Wielun area. 550lb and fragmentation bombs cut great swathes through the ranks of the unprotected horse soldiers and Dinort's Gruppe was followed by 30 more bombers from Schwarzkopff's I/StG77 which completed the decimation.

The story was repeated on the 2nd with Stukagruppen of LG2 making attacks at Dziloszyn in support of the XI Army and following these up with raids on Polish troop concentrations south-east of Tachenstachau. Forty Stukas from I/StG2 and I/StG76 surprised a Polish division of infantry detraining at Piotrkow railway station and wiped them out. Troop columns at Radomsko were cut up by StG77.

On the 3rd came the assault by the German Navy on the surviving ships of the Polish fleet sheltering at Hela. Two German destroyers,

Leberecht Maass and *Max Schultz*, attacked these vessels, the principal components of which were the minelayer *Gryf* (2,250 ton), the largest unit of the Polish fleet, and the destroyer *Wicher* (1,520 ton). Both the German destroyers were driven off and the Navy had no option but to call in the Stukas. All the Luftwaffe Gruppen were now fully engaged in support of the Army, but 11 of the Navy Stuka unit, 4/186, were operational and these were sent in against the two Polish ships that morning.

They scored several near misses on the minelayer and one hit which penetrated her quarterdeck, but the ship remained afloat. In a final attack that afternoon the Navy divebombers had more luck, and although one of the Ju87s was shot down by flak the *Wicher* was sunk with two direct hits and the *Gryf* was hit again on her forward deck, the bomb piercing her magazines. The resulting explosion completely wrecked her and started fierce fires which spread to her oil fuel and burned for two days before the sank.

Below: With negligible fighter opposition the Stukas proved an outstanding success in the brief Polish campaign./*Ullstein*

Thus in a brief concentrated action the Ju87 brought home to one small Navy the effectiveness of the dive-bomber and the vulnerability of the small warship. Unfortunately the news of this action was slow filtering through to the west and each navy was in turn to learn the same lesson in the same manner in the ensuing years.

Meanwhile the land campaign was drawing to its inevitable conclusion, and despite fierce resistance by the Poles, the German Army was soon threatening the capital, Warsaw. The resulting action has been widely heralded as the first use of the Stuka as a 'terror weapon' and lurid stories began to appear in the Western Press of how the gallant undefended city had been subjected to merciless air attack.

In fact Warsaw had been turned into a very well defended fortress by the Polish Army who had every intention of fighting a desperate rearguard action, street by street, through the city. Despite repeated appeals to abandon the capital, which the Germans made in leaflet raids, 100,000 men entrenched themselves, ready to carry out this plan. It was a brave but futile gesture, for already the Soviet Army had stabbed them in the back and was flooding across her eastern frontiers and in the west not one British or French soldier had taken a step forward to take the pressure off their gallant ally.

Goering ordered Richthofen to smash the defenders' resistance and will to continue and thus avoid a lengthy campaign; the Germans were still nervous about their exposed rear and wished to transfer men and aircraft to the Western Front as soon as possible. Thus it was that at dawn on 15 September an air fleet

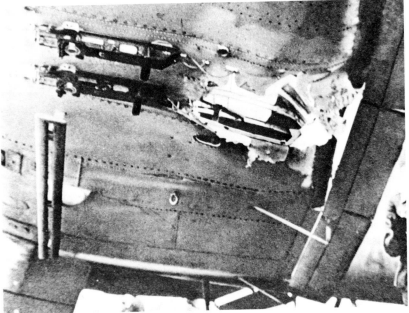

of some 400 aircraft commenced a continual bombardment of the city defences. Because the bulk of the medium bombers were already in transit west, by far the greater percentage of the aircraft involved in this attack were Stukas. Two hundred and forty of them in all, from eight Gruppen, supported by a motley collection of Junkers Ju52 transports and auxiliary types. The whole day passed with repeated waves of dive-bombers passing over the city and releasing their cargoes of high-explosives into the inferno which was stoked by incendiary raids by Ju52s. Kesselring later recorded:

'I often visited the Stuka squadrons on their return from bombing raids over Warsaw, spoke with the crews about their impressions and inspected the damage where aircraft had been hit by flak. It was almost a miracle that some of them got home, so riddled were they with holes—halves of wings were ripped off, bottom planes were torn away, and fuselages disembowelled, with their control organs hanging by the thinnest threads. Our thanks were due to Dr Koppenberg and his engineers who produced such aircraft as the Ju87 which was still in use in Russia in 1945.'*

The following day the Stukas were sent against Modlin and again on the 27th, but these demonstrations saved much worse destruction which street fighting would have brought. On 27 September the Poles surrendered.

The Polish campaign had been a complete vindication of the ground-support principle for which the Luftwaffe was now designed and it proved to be the blueprint for all subsequent German attacks and campaigns. Above all, it had been the Ju87 which had carried the day and the reputation they earned for themselves during September was to do much to overawe future opposition in the months ahead, and the whole victorious campaign had been achieved with the loss of only 31 of all the Stukas involved. It was an impressive début.

There followed, during the winter of 1939–40, a strange lull with very little action other than at sea. In fact Hitler had determined to

*From *The Memoirs of Field Marshal Kesselring*; William Kimber, London.

Top: Ground fire indeed proved more effective than fighters during the Polish campaign. On an airfield in East Prussia the crew of Ju87B examine the effects of a direct hit.
/*Archiv Schliephake*

Above: This is what happened! Airmen are the same the world over and this young pilot is no doubt elaborating to his comrades this piece of good luck!
/*Archiv Schliephake*

Left: Ground crew manhandling the next bomb load.
/*Archiv Schliephake*

Above right: Another significant quality of the Stuka was its ability to operate from the most primitive type of airstrip.
/*Archiv Schliephake*

Right: The Ju87B was the most widely used version in the opening stages of the war.
/*Archiv Schliephake*

26

unleash his forces against the Allies as soon as Poland had been crushed and his operational plans were duly prepared, but bad weather throughout that winter led to repeated postponements of the jumping-off date and by the early spring the Allies had convinced themselves that, in Prime Minister Chamberlain's words, 'Hitler has missed the bus'.

Nothing could have been farther from the truth, of course, but before the German Panzers crashed over the frontiers into France and the Low Countries the complacent Allies were to experience, at first hand, a small sample of what the Poles had suffered and what they were in for.

Hitler had long held uneasy doubts about the neutrality of Norway and the *Altmark* incident inflamed his fear that Britain intended to occupy that small nation and at one blow cut off vital iron-ore supply routes and his outlet to the Atlantic. In fact the British Government had no such notions but they had intended to land troops at Norwegian ports and march them across land to aid the Finns who were resisting a full-scale Russian invasion.

To forestall any such enterprise, real or imagined, the German Leader decided to occupy Norway himself in a surprise move and although the campaign, Operation Weseruebing, was to be mainly a naval affair with the whole of the German Navy committed to the invasion, airborne landings to seize vital airfields and to fly in quickly light reinforcements to hold key cities, meant that the Luftwaffe was also heavily involved. As an afterthought, and with future bombing

Right: Return from another mission. Stukas on an airfield during the Polish campaign. /*IWM*

Below: 'Gruppen scramble!' – a still from the German film 'Stukas'. Friedrich Lang recalls that on one occasion the Flag Guard stuck to his post for too long and was run down by a wayward Stuka taking off! /*Archiv Schliephake*

Bottom: Early example of a propaganda picture. This photo was faked from a shot taken over prewar Spain to illustrate a true incident which took place over the Baltic in 1939. A damaged Ju87C jettisoned its detachable undercarriage. This was blown up in the press handout to illustrate the sturdiness of the Ju87B which was alleged to have broken off its wheel fairings on striking the water in too low a dive. Many German pilots witnessed the true incident but this photo is pure fake. /*Archiv Schliephake*

missions against England at the back of his mind, Hitler decided to annex Denmark at the same time.

In view of Great Britain's supremacy at sea, surprise was to be a major factor in German planning, and to back up their sea and land forces Fliegerkorps X under the command of General Geisler was prepared for the Norwegian operations. This unit had been formed in the early months of 1940 from Fliegerdivision 10, which was the anti-shipping unit, and, in view of the expected retaliation from the Home Fleet, it was an apt choice. To coordinate all airborne transport operations a special staff named Transportchef Land was set up under control of Geisler.

On 9 April the forces available to the Germans comprised some 290 He111 and Ju88 bombers, 100 single- and twin-engined fighters, almost 500 transports from 11 Gruppen and 40 Stukas. To oppose this mass there was only the ill-prepared obsolete Norwegian Air Force and such weak forces which the Allies could scrape together and these came too late to affect the issue. Hitler was certain that the Allies would react sluggishly to any original idea and he was shown to be correct.

When the attack went in at 0500hrs on the 9th it was a crushing success. Land forces crossed the Danish frontier brushing aside weak resistance. Seaborne landings were made on the Danish islands and an impressive fly-past of airborne units on their way to

Norway had the desired effect. Denmark fell on the first day. The success in Norway, although widespread, was not so absolute.

Bf110 fighters swept over the airfields at Oslo/Fornebu and Stavanger/Sola annihilating most of the defending fighters either on the ground or in brief dog-fights, the most modern machines the stunned Norwegians had were Gloster Gladiators and so Goering's Zerstörer units had no difficulty. These attacks were followed by paratroop drops which also went mainly according to plan and by the evening of Day One both airfields were in use as Ju52s ferried in troops and supplies and the first twin-engined fighters and Stukas moved in. By 10 April 12 Ju87RS of 2/StGI and II were using Sola.

At sea the German invasion force had received a more severe battering and subsequent British naval operations almost wiped out the fledgling German Navy, which lost the heavy cruiser *Blücher* at Oslo to Norwegian shore defences, the light cruisers *Königsberg* and *Karlsrühe* and 10 big destroyers. But the British were not prepared for an occupation and before they could mount serious counter-measures the Germans became firmly established.

The first Stuka assault was put in by 1/StGI flying from Kiel/Holtenau. The fortress of Akershus and Oskarsborg, which barred the approaches to Oslo, had been putting up fierce resistance all morning and at 1059hrs, in an effort to finally silence these guns, Hauptmann Hozzel's Stukas were

sent against them and scored numerous hits.

Allied landings of hastily gathered ill-organised troops took place at the smaller ports in northern Norway during the period 16th–19th and the major port of Narvik was in dispute following the Royal Navy's victories there, but for the Allies this campaign, fought without air cover, consisted of a long, miserable series of retreats and reverses as the reinforced German Army fought its way up the spine of Norway and took all the coastal towns one by one.

The main effort of Fliegerkorps X was made against the landing ports of the Allied Expeditionary Forces and against the Allied warships at sea and in the fiords. At first only the medium bombers had the range to take part but they scored several impressive victories, Ju88s of II/KG30 being instrumental in hitting and causing heavy damage to the 8in cruiser *Suffolk* after she had bombarded Sola airfield. Thereafter the Home Fleet kept well to the north.

The main Stuka activity was in the ground-support rôle but as the German Army advance continued they had the opportunity to test their mettle against the anti-aircraft ships of the Royal Navy. Lack of defending aircraft or adequate anti-aircraft guns ashore had meant that various light cruisers and sloops with heavy AA capacity had been sent over from England to provide cover for the tiny harbours and the assembled transports at places like Namos, Narvik and Aandalsnes.

These ports, located miles from open water

Above: A Stuka crew rest between sorties at Stavanger/Sola airfield (the long-range fuel tanks of this 'Richard' have been scratched out on the negative). */Franz Selinger*

29

up narrow sheer-sided fiords, soon became death traps to shipping. Most of the Royal Navy's smaller warships, cruisers, destroyers and the like, were hopelessly under-armed when it came to dealing with air attacks and whereas this deficit could sometimes be compensated for out at sea by high-speed steaming and rapid manoeuvring, when locked in the fiords and subjected to repeated dive-bombing, losses began to mount.

It was not until the arrival of the Stukas of I/StG1 commanded by Hauptmann Paul-Werner Hozzel on the scene, however, that the warships' ordeal began in earnest. On 3 May an Allied force of transports, cruisers and destroyers evacuating the rearguard troops from Namos was located by dive-bombers at 0845hrs while still withdrawing, and the French destroyer *Bison* (2,435 ton) was hit and set on fire. Numerous troops were killed by the explosion and the subsequent fire and she had to be sunk. While hurrying to catch up with the rest of the force which had gone on ahead, the British destroyer *Afridi* (1,820 ton), one of the largest and newest destroyers at sea, was located by three Stukas who concentrated on her. The *Afridi* was the flotilla leader's ship of the 4th Flotilla under the command of Capt Philip Vian, 'Vian of the *Cossack*' as he was already known, and he gave a vivid description of the confusion of her last moments:

'On reaching Admiral Cunningham's force at 1400hrs we expected to be able to relax, since good offing had been made and the convoy would, we hoped, be outside the range of the dive-bombers. This was not so; a formation of Stukas arrived simultaneously with us. One

Top: Stab 1/StG1 with Ju87Rs ('Richards') on a Norwegian base./*Archiv Schliephake*

Above: Stuka operative from a frozen lake in Norway arouses interest from two pretty Norwegian 'hosts'. /*Archiv Schliephake*

Left: With the added flexibility of the long-range fuel tanks the Ju87Rs were able to range out into the fiords and here they found many sitting targets. A stick of bombs lands close alongside the repair ship *Vindictive* at the main Allied base of Harstad./*IWM*

Above right: The most efficient anti-aircraft defence against the Stuka the Allies had, was the 40mm Bofors gun. Here an army Bofors crew awaits the next dive-bomber attack on Namos, and the crowded anchorage./*IWM*

Right: A few Stukas were fitted with ski landing gear in Norway, but the experiment was *not* a success./*Ullstein*

30

of them went into a dive on our starboard side, its target obviously *Afridi*. The vital action was taken, a violent turn towards the plane, to make the angle of descent too steep for the pilot. At this point Gammon reported a second Stuka coming at us from the port side. Maurice suggested reversing the rudder but I thought this would bring the ship up steady just about the time the bombs arrived, and I asked him to continue to turn to starboard.'*

This proved fatal and the scudding destroyer was hit by two bombs. The first struck just abaft the bridge structure and penetrated the forward boiler-room, starting a heavy fire and causing numerous casualties, while the second landed on the fo'c'sle and tore away a large part of the hull. The fire quickly spread and all way was lost, an attempt to take her in tow was abandoned and she went down with the loss of 49 officers and men, 13 soldiers and 30 of *Bison*'s survivors.

But it was the ships penned up in the fiords which were to suffer most from the Stukas' dive-bombing attacks. One of the largest and most valuable victims to fall to the dive-bombers at this time was the Polish troopship *Chrobry* (11,442 ton). She was carrying additional troops to reinforce Bodö escorted by the destroyer *Wolverine* and the sloop *Stork*, but was caught by I/StG1 and subjected to heavy attacks. Hit by one 550lb bomb she caught fire and sank on 15 May.

By far the most well provided for ships in the Royal Navy at that time were the AA

*From *Action This Day*; memoirs of Adm Sir Philip Vian, Muller, London.

sloops of the Black Swan class, which mounted three twin 4in guns and a multiple pom-pom. They were in great demand throughout the campaign, as a result of which they suffered heavily. At Aandalsnes the *Black Swan* herself was subjected to non-stop Stuka attack throughout both the 26th and 27th, surviving innumerable assaults and shooting away over 1,000 rounds of 4in ammunition in the course of a single day. Eventually with ammunition low and her gunners exhausted, she was ordered to withdraw and Capt Poland took her down the fiord to safety. At 1600hrs the Ju87s pounced again.

'For the hundredth time I shouted down the voice-pipe to the transmitting station, "Open fire, pom-pom". In the brilliant sunlight I could see the pilot clearly as the bomb was released at masthead height; then the aircraft zoomed away, surrounded by tracer bullets. I looked aft and my heart went cold. I gained a split-second impression of guns on duty at the after mounting, gazing open-mouthed up at the descending horror, then I saw it hit the quarter-deck just below him. A little puff of smoke went from the wooden deck, and that was all.'*

The *Black Swan* had in fact suffered a miraculous escape for the bomb, released too low, had passed straight through the quarter-deck, down through the wardroom, through a fresh water tank, on down into the after 4in magazine, passed between the ship's twin propeller shafts and out through the ship's bottom before exploding on the bottom of the fiord where the water muffled the worst effects of the blast. Not all ships had such phenomenal luck.

Her sister ship, the *Bittern*, was caught in similar circumstances on 30 April at Namos. All day she had been pounded by relays of Stukas determined to rid that port of its sole protection, and in so doing they afforded the hard-pressed troops ashore some respite. But it could not go on for ever and in the late afternoon a formation of three dive-bombers came in, two from ahead and the third from over her stern, thus effectively splitting her limited defences.

The two coming in over the bows were beaten off, but the third Stuka planted his bomb right aft on the little vessel and detonated a steel locker holding demolition charges. With a roar and a sheet of flame the entire stern was blown away. The depth-charge stowage threatened to explode and add to the inferno and Lt-Cdr Mills was forced to abandon ship. The *Bittern* was finally sunk by torpedo from the destroyer *Juno*, once her fires had got out of hand.

*From *Stand by for Action*, by Cdr W. Donald, published by William Kimber, London.

Thus it was that with German aerial dominance, all the precarious beachheads established by the Allies in Norway fell until only Narvik remained. Although his great offensive in France was imminent Hitler was still obsessed with the importance of this port and urged his commanders to greater efforts to retake the town. Bombing already heavy, was further stepped up and by 10 June, with disaster facing them in the south, the Allies bowed to the inevitable and the remaining soldiers were taken off by the Navy and Narvik fell into German hands.

The whole campaign had shown the importance of air power even in areas where control of the sea lay in other hands. The Allies, ill-prepared and confused, could do nothing to stem such a coordinated onslaught, but by the time the last British soldier had sailed away from Norway, this country had already been relegated to the back pages of the newspapers. The Western Front had burst asunder and the Stukas were leading the German legions towards the peak of their achievements.

Top: In Norway in 1940 the Royal Navy first learned the power of the dive-bomber. The anti-aircraft sloop *Bittern* burns steadily after taking a direct hit aft./*IWM*

Above: Her stern a tangled mass of metal and debris the *Bittern* drifts down the fiord after a Stuka assault./*IWM*

3 Race to the Sea

The brief annihilating land campaign opened by Germany on 10 May 1940, proved to be the culmination of her techniques started in Spain and perfected in Poland. Against this new concept of warfare, thrusting armour columns, mechanised infantry and continuous air support, the armies of Belgium, France and the BEF melted away like snow and within 48 hours of the initial bomber strikes on Dutch, Belgian and French airfields, the whole situation was clearly out of the hands of the Allied commanders. The rout which followed was catastrophic; within five days Holland had surrendered. Belgium offered more resistance but the Allies had been outwitted, outflanked and outfought by the German thrust through the Ardennes.

After the first long-range strikes which destroyed the bulk of the Allied air strength as it lay deployed on its runways, the majority of the 1,100 medium bombers available to Luftflotten 2 and 3 were switched to troop support, but it was the Stukas, 320 of which were deployed along the fronts, which again proved to be the key to the campaign, although they were still used to attack targets in the rear of the Allied lines rather than in direct support of the troops.

Fliegerkorps VIII, commanded by von Richthofen, was operating at the peak of its efficiency, mounting up to nine sorties a day for each aircraft, and moving forward rapidly from one improvised airstrip to another to keep up with the pell-mell advances of the armoured columns. Whenever an Allied artillery or infantry concentration, or tank formation, started to offer serious resistance to the advancing Panzers, the German liaison officers whistled up the Stukas, which then smashed it and enabled the advance to continue. Even the Germans were surprised at the degree with which the British and French armies were paralysed by such methods.

Everywhere the whine and howl of the Ju87 was the signal for the collapse of the defence and the penetration of the racing tanks. In Holland, the vital Maas citadel of Eban Emael was taken by audacious airborne assault and the Stukas of StG2 contributed by pulverising Belgian troops massing for a counter-attack, and at Moerdijk Ju87s had destroyed defence works and flak positions guarding the vital viaducts over the Diep, which were taken and held by paratroops soon afterwards.

Dietrich Peltz was to achieve lasting fame later in the war, his missions ranging from bombing missions with KG77 in the Battle of Britain and Russia, through the Bomber Unit at Foggia and Tours in 1942 to attacks with rocket-assisted bombs against shipping in the Arctic and the Mediterranean, finally ending the war as the commanding general of Fliegerkorps I. But it was as a Stuka leader that he first made his name, joining the 'Immelmann' Geschwader in April 1936, and subsequently serving with I/StG162, I/StG167 and, finally, I/StG76 in May 1939. He was the Kapitän of the first Staffel at the time of the Neuhammer disaster. With this group (re-numbered as 1/StG3 in July 1940) Peltz flew some 102 combat sorties in the Polish and French campaigns without a single loss. On one of the French missions,

Left: Maj Graf Schönborn, the so-called 'Stuka Father' because of his age. He led StG77 in France, the Battle of Britain and on the Eastern Front./*Ullstein*

33

Peltz's group was assigned the task of supporting an airborne landing as this contemporary account describes:

'The first duty of Peltz's squadron was to cover the transports' mission with bombs and machine gun fire in order to eliminate any possibilities of flak. Soon after take-off Peltz found the transports in a meadow close by a large estate, further transports, overtaken by the faster Stukas of his unit, were still landing there and Peltz circled the area at a height of 50m. He could see the infantrymen getting out of the transports below, getting a table from the main house (Peltz couldn't believe his eyes at this), next a pure white tablecloth and straight after that the infantrymen got a hearty breakfast from the house! Peltz could see all this quite plainly from the height he was circling.

'This was supposed to be the war in the west with all its horrors? He could hear in his earphones the disgusted remarks his men were making about the so-called "Shooting" war, their thoughts were the same as his own. The Oberleutnant climbed up higher to have a wider look round the area. In the whole of the wider surroundings of the estate he could see no military points worth shooting at, only a solitary local observer, a Henschel Hs126, waved its wings in greetings to the Stukas. From his experience in the Polish campaign Peltz knew that these local observers had more than once given the Stukas some good targets. "We could not talk to each other, as the observer was on a different frequency, so one just stuck close to him and waited. He flies in a loop and the navigator waves. Aha, there is a target after all, that friendly observer has taken us to

34

Above left: A Ju87B of 'Immelmann' Geschwader in 1940./*Ullstein*

Centre left: 100kg bombs and dive brake detail./*Franz Selinger*

Bottom left: Armourers at work on the bomb crutch of a Stuka. /*Bundesarchiv*

Above: The gaunt outline of the Stuka at rest./*Archiv Schliephake*

an airfield. There is a hangar but we could see no planes at all. Therefore we shoot up the hangar, hopefully there might be something worthwhile coming out of it. Nothing! The Staffel flies home, both pilots and radio operators are completely amazed. Never before had it happened that they had returned from a combat mission with all their bombs still aboard.'' The only consolation they had from this abortive operation was that the Staffel from the Gruppe Sigel had exactly the same experience.

'During the afternoon the Staffel takes-off on a similar mission, but again there is nothing on. No military targets in sight. On their way back they saw the first German vehicles at the Luxembourg-Belgian border. A huge column moving slowly along the roads to the west and the south-west, in parts they are four abreast. The Stuka crews felt unease for their comrades on the ground when they thought of attacks by enemy aircraft against such a mass. But as far as they could see nothing was happening. "You could hardly believe it, but you couldn't get away from it." Again the squadron returned with all their bombs and all their ammunition from this mission. The ground crew NCO said, disgustedly, "Don't we need any bombs any more!" and the men from the ground personnel refused to speak to the aircrews so disappointed were they. This marked the end of the second mission of 10 May 1940, the day when the German army left their winter quarters at the Westwall to go into battle in France and Flanders. The poor Stuka crews laid down on the straw as disappointed as the other men who wouldn't even speak to them.

'On 11 May operation maps showed that the point of the army was deep into Belgium. "In the morning we got the operation command together with our target. A group of villages, a point the army had met strong resistance, and the Stukas were to break it." They flew as in peacetime at a height of 2,000m looking for the enemy, but they couldn't see anything over the target zone at all. They therefore dived down and flew over it again at about 10m height. They still could see nothing of the enemy. The village was obviously evacuated, there was nobody in the streets, no cattle or animals in the fields. On his own responsibility Peltz flew another 50km to the west. Nothing!

'Hedgehopping they flew back. Finally, on a beautiful tarmac road, the advance guard of the army came into view. Armoured scout cars and other vehicles stopped at the side of the road. Here also it looked just like peacetime. The soldiers sat in the ditches eating their breakfasts. Only from the markings could you see that they were German vehicles and from that it could be assumed that the war was still on!

'For the third time the Staffel brought its bombs back. The men jumped disgusted from their planes. The ground crew hardly looked at them. And they are supposed to be dive-bombers! Peltz interrogated each one of his men. Not one of them had seen even a single enemy soldier.

'Then came the order for them to carry out an attack on the fortification of Neuchapel. After Modlin these were the first bunkers that heavy Stuka bombs had fallen on, but the Staffel was very surprised for there was no defence. Also outside the bunkers themselves there was no enemy in sight at all.

35

'The next attack was meant for an enemy column on the roads to Fort Givet. Each Staffel was assigned one road. At last a worthwhile target! These columns of troops just had to be there, nobody could just imagine them. Nothing there. The roads were empty. Without fighter cover the Stukas flew close to Givet. Peltz flew on ahead of the group following the road, now he felt just too stupid. He made a long loop and retraced his course to a small wood where he dropped a few small bombs at random. That made things lively. The smoke from the bombs had hardly reached the tops of the trees when from the wood came galloping horses, soldiers, soldiers and soldiers again. "You see", Peltz shouted into his microphone, "Who says!" The Staffel attacked, shooting into the woods, into people and animals below, whatever they had. That knocking with the small bombs at the woods had been well worthwhile!'

The preparations for the reduction of Fort Eben Emael were practised with great detail and patience during the early months of 1940, as the Kommandant of the Stuka unit involved, II/StG77, recalled to the author: 'At Schweinfurt we and the special paratroop team received our orders for the taking of Fort Eben Emael. From February 1940, both units were placed under the strictest security and only at 0200hrs on the morning of 10 May 1940 could I actually give the operational command. Indeed, on the 9 May, my Kommodore, Günter Schwartzkopff, and I were still at Lippstadt, where our training camp was established, taking examinations for young flyers in our units, when we received the operational command for the next day!

'The operation against such a pin-point target in a very limited area right next to the previously landed gliders and paratroops did not only call for accuracy, but our crews also carried a heavy responsibility to our comrades on the ground and the success of the whole offensive.

'We exercised as in peacetime, and no one except me knew which target was next. When the Air Command proposed the use of live bombs on training sessions with the paratroops on the ground, I declined and pointed out that an accidently wrong placement of live weapons would only spoil morale for both units in the later, real, operation. They agreed with me and we practised with the normal cement training bombs.'

In the Netherlands too, the dive-bombers were able to influence events at sea, for by the second day of the campaign British and French destroyers were working off the Dutch coast, evacuating the Dutch Royal Family and gold

reserves and bringing over demolition parties to deny the Germans the installations and fuel supplies at Ijmuiden, the Hook, Flushing and Antwerp.

The Dutch Navy took a beating as well. When the German troops established themselves on the island of Waalhaven and took its airfield, the destroyer *Jan Van Galen* was despatched to bombard them and drive them out. It was a forlorn hope, similar to the *Suffolk*'s bombardment of Sola, but it was gallantly carried out. The destroyer arrived off the airfield at midday on the 10th, while the lumbering Ju52 transports were still arriving, and managed to destroy no less than three of them with anti-aircraft fire. She then turned her four 4·7in guns on the German troop emplacements ashore and for over an hour laid down a heavy barrage. Retribution was not long delayed, however, and 32 dive-bombers—a whole Gruppe—were sent out to deal with her.

In many ways the tiny Netherlands Navy was way ahead of the Royal Navy in the field of anti-aircraft defence, and the destroyers of the Witte de With class, although 10 years old, mounted one 2·9in heavy AA gun and four 40mm Bofors as well as four 12·7mm light guns. Compare this with the typical defence system carried by the modern Javelin class of the Royal Navy, which had just entered service in 1939. These vessels carried only one pom-pom mounting and two quadruple 0·5in machine guns and they were well

Above: A faked photograph purporting to show a Stuka in a dive during the 1940 campaign in France./*Ullstein*

Above right: Hidden in the woods, a Stuka lies dormant awaiting the call to strike. /*Archiv Schliephake*

equipped compared with most destroyers. Moreover, the staff at the DNO had only recently stated that, in their opinion, eye-shooting weapons were adequate for air defence. The Dutch destroyer was fitted with the Hazemeyer fire-control instruments and the guns and directors were fully stabilised by gyros.

Even so, despite her superior equipment, the *Jan Van Galen* found the odds of 32 to one too much; she received a direct hit which so damaged her that she had to be abandoned in a sinking condition. The German occupation then continued without further interruption.

Much the same fate overcame the gunboat *Johan Maurits Van Nassau* four days later. On 13 May the Germans had established a battery of guns opposite the Dutch fortifications at Kornwerdzand on the Zuider Zee dike. The gunboat crept in under cover of heavy morning mists on the seaward side and her three 5·9in guns thereupon silenced the German position. She too was caught by the dive-bombers when she endeavoured to escape to sea the following day and was quickly sunk.

Waldemar Plewig, leading II/StG77, describes the breakneck pace of the advance across Western Europe in the summer of 1940:

'After the successful operation against Eben Emael our wing was transferred to Holland, moving into various advanced airfields as the fighting progressed. Thanks however to the very good organisation of Gen Pflugbeil and the ever ready efficiency of our two aerodrome service squadrons, strengthened by the workers battalion of young men under the service age group, but with technical qualifications, we could very quickly follow up our advances and provide forward Panzers with badly needed and often requested close air support, but initially our wing was held back from the immediate operations in support of the army and held in reserve for the Fliegerkorps Richthofen.

'During the advance on, and operations over, Dunkirk, we gave vital support, and during this phase had our first losses in this campaign. One of my crews had to crash land in enemy territory, but they destroyed their aircraft and were promptly rescued by another crew. At Dunkirk two of our crews were shot down by ship's anti-aircraft guns mounted on a troopship, but the ship itself was soon subsequently sunk.

'Further operations, when we crossed the Maginot Line, also called for greater precision from our pilots as we had to drop the bombs just in front of our own troops amongst the guns. One special task we were given at this time, when we could not see any targets, we had the responsibility to locate and attack any French tanks we could find, which were usually well hidden in farmyards and the like. We had some considerable success in this with the newly developed fragmentation

Above: Striking force. A powerful force of Ju87Bs crosses the flat French plains spearheading another attack in 1940. /*Bundesarchiv*

bombs, for although the French tanks could stand up to all but direct hits, we could simply immobilise them by damaging their tracks, which put them out of the fight.'

On the 12th the British flotilla leader *Codrington* evacuated the Dutch Crown Princess and her family, from Ijmuiden and on the following day Queen Wilhelmina and her suite were snatched from under the noses of the advancing Germans by the destroyer *Hereward*. This intensely annoyed Hitler who had ordered their capture. Also on the 13th another British destroyer, the *Windsor*, evacuated the Dutch Government. All this was not accomplished without loss, however.

The Stukas were now taking the opportunity to strike hard at the stream of vessels pulling out of Holland, and among their targets were the escorting British destroyers. Many of these were the ancient V and W types, but despite their age they performed magnificent work. Several of them had been converted to act as AA ships with twin 4in guns replacing their former armaments. Even so the Ju87 was able to pierce this type of barrage with ease, and on the 15th the *Valentine* was hit while attempting to protect one of the Scheldt ferries. Badly knocked about, she was beached at the mouth of the Scheldt and abandoned. During the ensuing two days, both the *Winchester* and *Westminster* were hit and damaged, while on the 19th the dive-bombers caught the *Whitley* and so damaged her that she ran aground between Nieuport and Ostend and was lost.

After the initial walkover of 10 and 11 May the advancing Germans finally ran into some degree of resistance which the Stukas were called upon to break for them in the now classic manner:

'After the German tanks got though Bouillon they met with resistance from the French. The Staffel of Oberstleutnant Peltz was picked to break it. It was very early in the day, the ground was covered with fog and only the tops of hills were visible. Slowly the fog lifted and, flying over a wood, Peltz saw below him a vast number of vehicles. But, even though flying very low, he could not ascertain whether they were the enemy or our own, so he could not attack. On landing he was greeted with a message, that came from our leading tanks, that the French had counter-attacked with numerous vehicles. Were those he had sighted French after all? The Staffel flew back to the same spot with the order that, "If there are no vehicles on the road between Bouillon and Sedan they were to attack bunkers marked X" At a height of 3,000m the Staffel arrived at the appointed area. It had become a beautiful summer's day. far below the Stukas stretched the road. Peltz went down to 2,000m, and then 1,500m to check the road and the surrounding countryside.

'Suddenly a shout. "Alert, fighters behind us. "This call, heard for the first time in the French invasion, acted like a fanfare. It was for the Stuka crews, their first meeting with enemy fighters in the west. But there was no time for any thoughts on the matter, already their gunfire was cutting through the Staffel's

formation. The radio operators fired back with every gun that could bear. By this time they were almost over Sedan. Far below lay the fortifications for which their bombs were intended. In spite of constant attacks from the fighters, which could only be fought off by the rear gunners, the Staffel dropped their bombs. With the superiority of the French fighters there was now only one thing left to do – go home at full speed. The French followed for some time and then a delighted yell in the earphones – one of the French fighters was hit and was crashing to the ground. If this loss shocked the French, or if they were by this time running short of fuel was not clear. But one thing was clear to the Stuka crews, after the shooting down they showed their bellies with the big cockades on the undersides of their wings and flew off.

'Only now did Peltz have time enough to check on his unit. Two planes were missing. This served only as confirmation of what he had already witnessed. During the brief air battle one of the Ju87s dived away with smoke coming out of it. Peltz slowed down to let the rest of the Staffel pass him by. By checking the aircraft markings he could tell that one of the missing men was Oberstleutnant Haller. At this moment the Staffel flew over the first of the German lines and Peltz saw a high column of smoke rising from the ground. This would not have been an unusual event to notice from the front line, for there was burning in lots of places, but Peltz felt that this was more. He went down lower and there was a Ju87 burning fiercely. It was Haller's

machine. He had managed, even with a badly damaged machine, to get to his own lines. Peltz went down even lower and saw Haller, his face as black as coal, waving fiercely.

'Haller appeared to be uninjured, but his gunner was laying against a tree and not moving. "We must get help, but how?" Then Peltz had a brainwave when he observed marching infantry on the road near the aerodrome. He climbed to gain some room and then wrote quickly on a piece of paper, "Wounded pilot 300m west from the road near burning plane, please help!" He put the piece of paper in a pouch, dived back down towards the infantry, who twisted their necks to watch a pilot making pretty aerobatics above them. A few metres in front of the battalion Peltz drops the pouch trailing a string of penants behind it and can observe some of the infantrymen running to pick it up. If it is possible to help the wounded man he will be alright now, as with every infantry battalion there is always a doctor.

'While Peltz following his Staffel, disappearing to the north he mused on the fate of the other aircraft. As far as he can tell it is the Kettenhund leader Oberstleutnant Unbehauen. He couldn't believe it, that something could have happened to this sun bird whose nickname in the staffel is "Zaratza". Peltz landed, depressed to think that already this first air battle has cost him two losses. Two good crews missing, one Oberstleutnant Haller whose plane he saw burning on the ground, the other Oberst-

Above: The bomb release fork can clearly be seen in this photograph./*Archiv Schliephake*

39

leutnant Unbehauen, about which he knows nothing at all. Even though he knew other units had suffered losses from the French fighters this does not help.

'Then Peltz was called to the phone. And who was it at the other end, cheerful as always? "Zaratza," the sun bird! "Hello boss. I landed safely in German territory, with 65 bullet holes I'm sorry to say. Could you send me a Storch? Petrick got two stomach wounds. Landing facilities are so-so but if I was able to land my Ju87 you can land a Storch easily." "I'll fly myself", Peltz replied shouting. "In less than a quarter of an hour I'll be with you." Now everything has to be quick.

'The Storch was already standing with its engine running. Some bright person who had overheard the telephone conversation and guessed what was wrong. The Oberstleutnant rushed to the little plane just as he was. The door is slammed behind him and off he goes. The crash landing, the second Peltz has witnessed today, is quickly found. If you know the location, on an open field a Ju87 is hardly invisible. Here he found almost an identical picture to that presented by Haller's crash. The only difference is that "Zaratza's" plane is in one piece. The navigator was laying in the grass near the plane and the pilot waves. The similarity to the situation he witnessed only minutes before with Haller that only while he was landing did Peltz realise that "Zaratza" is not black in the face as Haller was.

'A few metres away from the Ju87 Peltz stopped the Storch and jumped out. Unteroffizier Petrick was lying very still and pale on his back. He appeared unconscious, his flying suit full of blood. "We'll sit him in the middle, you take his bottom and hold on to him. Get on 'Zaratza'!"

'Gently they carried the wounded man the few steps to the Storch. Unbehauen gets in first and pulls the Unteroffizier with his arms around his chest, after him, while Peltz lifts him from beneath. Petrick moaned. At last they got him on the seat where he collapsed. "Zaratza" held him up from behind with his arms.

'Sixty-five minutes after he received his two bullet wounds, Petrick is on the operating table. He's alright now. The doctors agreed that without his quick move to the field hospital he would not have been saved. Only then did Unbehauen find time to report to his leader exactly what happened to them in the air battle.

'Petrick must have received the wounds right at the beginning of the attack. I saw tracer all around in my cockpit, and heard noises in the engine and Petrick did not shoot. "Shoot man shoot" I called to him, and the poor devil gets up and shoots as I

have never seen him shoot before, five drums of ammunition he gave that French fighter. Then he collapsed. Especially for Petrick, with the nickname "Target" we gave him on account of his pot belly, and here they really had used it as a target.'

Meanwhile, conditions on the main front had, for the Allies, been deteriorating from bad to worse. By the evening of 12 May the Armoured Groups under Generals Guderian and Reinhardt had reached the Meuse near Sedan and were poised to thrust across. Stuka attacks were made at 1600hrs on the 13th against the French fortifications barring the approaches, and the Panzers crossed. Farther west, at Doncherry, 200 sorties were flown by Stuka units including StG77 commanded by Oberst Günter Schwarzkopff, so-called 'Stuka father', and by the 14th the 2nd Panzer Division was over.

The 'Grazer Gruppe', as StG76 was nicknamed, was the spearhead of the German attacks which crossed at Sedan and, under the overall command of Walter Sigel, were instrumental in making that spectacular advance possible. After Peltz's early encounters with French fighters, the Stukas more and more found themselves harried in this manner. The following account by Josef Grabler, is typical of the fierce fighting during that period:

'The breakthrough to Sedan was accomplished The German Panzers swung to the right and succeeded in their now historic advance to the sea at Abbeville, but the French tried very hard to attack these tank columns from the flanks and the rear. Now the Stukas were heavily involved in missions in support of the German advance. Typical of these was the attack on Chémery.

Above: Battle formation, Ju87Bs on patrol./*Archiv Schliephake*

Above right: Ground crew 'cranking up' a Stuka engine in France./*Archiv Schliephake*

'In the operational briefing they were instructed that on no account were they to attack tanks after 12 noon around Chémery. The German staff had calculated that by that time their own tanks would be through that town, and by putting this time limit on the Stuka attacks, hoped to prevent any attack being put in against their own units.

'On arrival over the battlefield at Chémery Peltz could see a whole lot of tanks, but, on account of the dust they were throwing up he was unable to recognise any of their markings. Peltz formed his Staffel into a defensive circle and then himself flew down to see if they were friend or foe. While thus engaged the cry "Fighters coming from the sun." Peltz climbed straight back to rejoin his Staffel and saw the white vapour trails of the enemy high in the sky above them. One Ju87 trailed smoke and Peltz saw with shock that it was the Commander's. Over the radio he ordered, "Squadron collect at Sedan", The Commander's plane was emitting smoke heavily and Peltz placed himself and his Staffel around him to shield him from further attack.

'Suddenly a French Morane appeared straight up in front of them exposing himself thus to the concentrated fire of all the static guns in their wings. The Frenchman exploded. In the meantime the Stukas saw, to their great delight, the arrival of German fighters. In front of the Stukas one of the Moranes was taken apart by the German fighters, as if for breakfast. This Frenchman also fell apart. After escorting the Commander as far as Sedan and safety over their own territory, the Staffel collected again. Later they found that the CO's gunner, Oberleutnant Herzog, had been killed by two cannon shots. Maj Sigel himself had received a grazing shot on his neck, but, luckily for him it only left a

burn blister, and, even though his machine was shot through like a sieve, he got home safely.

'From the rendezvous over Sedan the Staffel returned once more to Chémery, but they had hardly arrived back over the battlefield before the troublesome Moranes were back. Another air battle ensued, this time without effect to either side. Again the Stukas re-grouped in the skies above Sedan, and for the third time they returned to Chémery.

' "In front of us lies a small town. There are fierce fires and huge columns of smoke rise up. From the town countless tanks are going towards the German lines. They can only be French." Peltz therefore got ready to attack, behind him the whole Staffel dived in unison, In his bomb sights he had the group of tanks,

Above: Last checks before take-off./*Archiv Schliephake*

41

Above: Ease of maintenance in the field during fast flowing campaigns enabled the Stukagruppen to keep up a high sortie rate in France./*Ullstein*

thinking sometimes "Shall I release a 250 or will a 50kg be enough?" Each bomb release was watched closely by his comrades and criticised over the radio and those who missed were given the name "Watchmaker". When their bombs were all used up the pilot and gunner shot with their machine guns into the crowds of troops.'

Against fortifications only direct hits could demolish most of the forts but the Stuka bombs had another effect which proved just as valuable as one Kommandant describes: 'When around Namur, a fortification could not be taken by the ground troops despite every effort, we got the command to attack the Command Bunker itself with bombs. For this operation I called up our reserve squadron from Lippstadt so that our pilots who had not yet been in combat could have a try. After about 20 bombs we saw a white flag, and it all ended very quickly after an exchange between the "Top Brass" of both sides and our corps gave permission for the French Captain to leave with his sword on him. He said that his troops had to surrender for they could not stand any more of the shock waves caused by our bombs.'

a few more seconds and he would press his bomb release. Once his bomb is released the others will do the same! It is at this juncture that he recognised the swastika markings. Immediately he broadcast his warning. "Don't release. Our tanks!" This last-second command given during the dive was successful. Not one of the Staffel released. Despite the three air battles that he had just participated in all his men were alert enough to comply with that last-second order given in full dive, and the deadly drop on their brothers below was averted.

'When the Stukas finally landed it was found that as a result of the air battles several of the machines were very badly damaged. The outstanding casualty was one Ju87, its oxygen bottle hit by a cannon shell and exploded. While airborne everything inside this machine was loose, she came completely apart inside. The Leitwerk was only hanging on the wheel mountings by a shred and when she landed it literally disintegrated. No one was hurt.'

' "The type of war that had become classical in Poland, began again. With bombs and machine guns we attacked the convoys of vehicles. The enemy had terrible losses through the work of the Stukas. The enemy fighters appeared less and less, so that the Stukas could fly without fighter cover and could themselves hunt freely. Sometimes it was sheer target practice." Peltz recalled

All-out efforts by the Advanced Striking Force of the RAF and the medium bombers of the French Air Force to annihilate this bridge-head were met by strong fighter cover and devastating flak, and the Allied bomber formations were cut to ribbons. By the end of the day the German troops had little or nothing to fear from the air and their advance accelerated still further.

Punching through the disintegrating Allied armies, the Panzers reached the mouth of the Somme at Abbeville on the 20th and had surrounded and cut off the BEF with the main bulk of the French northern armies. They only needed to tighten these pincers and they could destroy these forces piecemeal. Boulogne was threatened and again it fell upon the hard-worked destroyers of the Dover flotillas to carry out evacuation and demolition work in the face of the Luftwaffe.

The destroyers *Whitshed* and *Vimiera* escorted the 20th Guards Brigade to Boulogne to organise the defence of the town which the British hoped to hold, but preparations for possible demolition were also being made by Adm Ramsey from his headquarters at Dover. The threat of the complete elimination of the entire BEF was now looming, and already the possibility of lifting a few troops from the northern ports while there was still time, was being considered. Demolition teams were also taken to Calais and Dunkirk, and plans were made to land supplies through these ports for the besieged armies.

The first attempt to assemble supply shipping was made by the British and French, but when, on the 20th, heavy German bombing caused losses at the latter port, Adm Abrial decided to clear all the larger ships from the harbour. On the 21st the Stukas arrived to disrupt this traffic and the French lost the destroyer *L'Adroit*, the tankers *Salome* and *Niger* and the troopship *Pavon*.

The 2nd Panzer Division now struck north from the Canche and attacked the outer perimeter of Boulogne's defence works. Although the line held, it was clear that under such pressure the end could not be long delayed. The destroyer *Vimy* was sent over to land a party of 200 seamen to hold the dock area, and two more destroyers, *Keith* and *Whitshed*, arrived the same day. Both came under artillery fire as they docked, the *Keith* and *Vimy* both having their commanding officers killed on the bridges of their ships while embarking the wounded.

To provide some assistance to the hard-pressed defence, a flotilla of French destroyers, under Capt de Portzamparc in the *Cyclone*, moved in to give close supporting fire and these ships were joined on the morning of the 23rd by the *Keith*, *Vimy*, *Wild Swan* which fired on German gun positions, troop concentrations and even individual tanks. This was to no avail, and when the Germans took Fort de la Creche it was clear that the port was doomed, and its evacuation was ordered at 1730hrs that afternoon.

Evacuation started at 1830hrs, which coincided with the arrival of the first Stuka formations, operating at the extreme length of their range from airstrips to the east of St Quentin. Two Gruppen peeled off over the town and concentrated on the dock area and the bombarding ships outside. Luckily, a small formation of RAF fighters arrived at the same time and broke up the assault, but even so this was not enough and many Ju87s got through to hit and set on fire the French destroyer *Orage*, which later had to be scuttled. The *Frondeur* was also hit and disabled and the British destroyer *Whitshed* near-missed.

Surprisingly, although the harbour was full of shipping, no vessel was lost there, although bombs falling on the quayside close by the *Keith* and *Vimy* caused some casualties. Further destroyers were now sent in despite fierce fire from German guns, and by the morning of the 24th all the surviving British defenders had been embarked.

Calais was ordered to hold out in order to delay the German push towards Dunkirk where the main evacuation was now planned to take place. The destroyers were again used to ferry over reinforcements for the garrison and also provided fire support when possible

Above: Fitting a Stuka with a replacement engine in the field. /*Archiv Schliephake*

but there was little else they could do to assist.

That these bombardments were effective was evident from the enemy's great efforts to drive the destroyers away. The *Grafton*, *Greyhound*, *Wessex*, *Vimiera* and the Polish *Burza* were all employed on this work during the 23rd and an urgent appeal went out from the commander of the 10th Panzer Division, which was fighting its way into the town in the face of dogged resistance, for air support.

Operating from Guise was StG2 commanded by Maj Oskar Dinort, and although the Channel coast represented the extreme limit of their range, two Gruppen were ordered to deal with the troublesome ships. Although still without an established routine for hitting fast moving vessels, the Stukas were proving extremely effective at the job, and on arrival over the coast Dinort ordered his two Gruppe commanders, Haupt Hitschold and Haupt Brückers, to pick their targets and attack.

In their clover-leaf formation in threes, the 40 Ju87s peeled off and dived towards the tiny vessels below, and as they did so the destroyers accelerated and their creamy wakes cut tortuous patterns on the steel-plate sea. Despite its doubts as to its ability to hit destroyers at speed, StG2 completed its dive-bombing attacks and, although jumped by Spitfires, returned to base without loss. On the previous day, however, eight Ju87s had been shot down by Allied fighters. The British lost the *Wessex* and had the *Vimiera* and *Burza* badly damaged during these and subsequent attacks.

In Calais town itself fighting centred on the Citadel where the British rearguard turned down an offer to surrender. Guderian therefore requested Richthofen to smash the Citadel by Stuka attack, and on the 26th two heavy assaults were delivered; the first was made by StG77 led by Graf Schönborn and later StG2 completed the task. The attack by StG2 was described by Peltz later thus:

'In the meantime the left flank of the German army was marching towards Calais. The military fortifications of the town were the new targets of Peltz's unit. Even on the very first flight towards it the men saw something they will never forget. The British Isles in the beaming sunshine, so close you could almost touch it. Only a very small strip of water separated it from the mainland, and from that height one felt you could throw a stone across.

'Before the Stuka attack other bombers had attacked Calais. The town burned in many places. The Tommies were obviously falling back. The smoke from the town was blown by the wind to the south-east and therefore the Stukas had to mount their attack, not from the mainland but from the direction of the sea. Thus they had to cross the territory of the British fighters, which crossed the water from Dover and Folkestone in bare minutes to lay in wait for bounty. Peltz knew this fact and informed his pilots and navigators of the likelihood of such encounters. Thus when he flew at 3,500m height and crossed the coastline to the north-east of Calais to get out to sea he was on the lookout for enemy fighters.

'One should not speak of the devil. Like a bullet out of a pistol a Spitfire flew past Peltz from a very high height and, with an elegant move, set itself behind him. The English pilot did this so cleverly that, as he came out of that curve he was almost directly beneath him and behind the Leitwerk of the German. It wasn't necessary but half of his Staffel shouted "Spitfire behind *Anna*", *Anna* being the name of Peltz's aircraft. He knew this only too well. Peltz dived straight down, in the hope that the English flyer would follow him. After a short while Peltz braked to slow down his dive, and there was Tommy, who couldn't brake at high speed, passing by his side. "Cheerio my friend" shouted Peltz, "Maybe another time". But there was not another meeting between the two. Peltz had hardly finished his greeting when, from the same direction as the English machine, like a shadow, another machine shot by and Peltz just recognised the German cross. "Now

Above: Return to battle, four Stukas fully bombed up, set off for the target./*Bundesarchiv*

we are alright!" Peltz straightened his machine and looked down seeing the Me shoot down the Spitfire. The whole incident from sighting the Spitfire to its destruction took only seconds. And now the Stuka bombs began to drop like hailstones from the Ju87s on to the ships in the harbour. Individual hits could not be made out as there was smoke everywhere.'

The 10th Panzer Division then went in, and by 1645hrs the town of Calais was in its hands. To the encircled Allied troops in the ever-shrinking perimeter only the small port of Dunkirk remained to them, and very little time.

On the evening of 26 May Operation Dynamo was officially put into effect by Adm Ramsey, but in truth the evacuation from Dunkirk had been going on since the 20th and already some 27,000 'useless mouths' had been brought away. On this day it was finally realised that attempts by the southern armies to break through the weak German corridor had failed. An armoured thrust against Amiens was broken up by dive-bombers of StG1 supported by medium bombers; StG77 smashed French artillery shelling St Quentin; and Lord Gort, C-in-C of the BEF, was informed that the Admiralty hoped to evacuate 45,000 of his troops in the two days they estimated were left to his command.

On the same day, the 26th, as the first swarms of little ships, transports and destroyers started to pick up the exhausted soldiers from the harbour mole and beaches,

the Luftwaffe was ordered to make Dunkirk their priority target and Rundstedt's Panzers moved forward for the kill. On the 27th the evacuation got under way in earnest, hastened by the surrender of the Belgians. The Luftwaffe arrived early with dawn assaults by the Gruppen of KG1 and KG4, followed by KG54. By the time the first Ju87 units arrived over the target Dunkirk was a shambles, and Adm Ramsey had told all available warships, an anti-aircraft cruiser, nine destroyers and four minesweepers, to close the beaches and use their small boats to supplement the lifts being made by the cross-Channel steamers and drifters.

Despite all their efforts, only 7,500 men were brought away, and the Stukas sank the large French Channel steamer *Cote d' Azur*. RAF cover over the approaches to the beach-head was patchy and Adm Ramsey reported that: 'Full air protection was expected, but instead, for hours on end the ships off-shore were subjected to a murderous hail of bombs and machine gun bullets.'

The Official Naval Historian thought this unfair because many of the fighter interceptions took place inland out of sight of the evacuation fleet and bitter troops. German sources also stress the part played by the RAF, but in fact the British fighter arm was not totally committed, for Dowding was attempting to build up a reserve of fighters in readiness for the clash over Britain which he knew must follow.

Fate came to the assistance of the BEF, for throughout the 28th and 29th the Luftwaffe was hampered by bad weather – low cloud and rain and drizzle – over its airfields and the target zone, which both reduced the number of sorties flown and the effectiveness of those aircraft that got through. As a result the number of men lifted to safety gradually increased. But on the 29th the skies cleared and once more the German bombers renewed their dominance over the coast.

Bombing was carried out by all types throughout this day, and losses among the crowded shipping mounted alarmingly. LG1, equipped with the new Junkers Ju88, scored an impressive success by sinking the 6,900 ton *Clan MacAlister* which was laden with landing-craft sent over to assist in the evacuation. She was the largest ship used at Dunkirk and was bombed and set ablaze while loading. The destroyer *Malcolm* took off her survivors and the burning ship was abandoned after a second attack.

Impressive though this was, the greatest disaster to the rescue fleet took place a little later when no less than three Geschwader of Stukas attacked, around 1700hrs. They concentrated on the Dunkirk Mole which was packed with ships embarking troops. Five British and three French destroyers, three large steamers and six trawlers were berthed there, and against this compact group the Ju87s threw themselves.

The destroyer *Grenade* was hit by a heavy bomb which turned her slender hull into a charnel-house and, blazing fiercely, her mooring lines parted and she drifted into the fairway. Further internal explosions ripped

Above: Peel Off – a perfect air-to-air shot of a formation of Stukas changing their approach route into an attack formation. Note the bomb racks are empty so this is not prior to an actual attack although the method is the same./*Bundesarchiv*

45

Above: Dunkirk, May 1940. The arrival of the dive-bombers over the beaches resulted in heavy shipping losses for the Allies, but bad weather restricted the number of Stuka sorties. A Ju87B in classic pose./*IWM*

Above right: Dunkirk, June 1940. While the fuel tanks blaze two British destroyers manoeuvre off the Mole. Stuka attacks on 1 June caused severe losses among the evacuating warships, including several destroyers. /*IWM*

through the crippled ship and desperate attempts were made to get her clear of the harbour entrance. She eventually sank just off the harbour mouth and casualties were severe.

The French destroyer *Mistral* also suffered severely when a bomb smacked into the quayside alongside her. The blast and screaming fragments completely demolished her upperworks, while her two sister ships, both laden with 500 troops, were near-missed but undamaged.

The destroyer *Jaguar* was hit and badly damaged but managed to struggle clear of the harbour, as did the *Verity*, although she was damaged by grounding outside. The trawlers *Calvi* and *Polly Johnson* both received direct hits and disintegrated and the paddle-steamer *Fenella* with 600 soldiers aboard was both hit and near-missed and abandoned. Another paddle-steamer, the *Crested Eagle*, attempted to get clear but was caught and hit by a heavy bomb. Severe losses were inflicted on her complement and the troops crammed aboard and she drifted, blazing, towards the beaches.

This devastating attack brought all embarkation attempts from the mole to a complete halt. Other vessels working off the beaches were also badly knocked about, including two railway ships, the *Lorina* and the *Normannia*, both of which were sunk. Meanwhile, a message had been received by Adm Ramsey that because of this raid the mole was useless for further evacuation. This proved to be a false alarm but it caused the switching of the bulk of the ships en route to Dunkirk, to the beaches with the subsequent delays and slowing down of the loading rate.

The loss of the *Grenade* by air attack and the *Grafton* and *Wakeful* by E-boat torpedoes, coupled with the damage to the *Jaguar*, *Gallant*, *Greyhound* and *Intrepid*, meant that six of the Royal Navy's most modern destroyers were now out of action and the First Sea Lord decided that such losses could not be

permitted among such valuable vessels; consequently all the big modern ships of the G, H, I and J classes were withdrawn from the evacuation. By far the greater bulk of the evacuation was being performed by the destroyers and this meant a severe blow to Adm Ramsey and his staff. The following day, rain and fog prevented the bombers from operating, with a resultant lowering of casualties, and the newer destroyers were ordered back into the holocaust.

They arrived back off the beaches on 1 June – and so did the Stukas. The latter's arrival coincided with a gap of three hours between the RAF patrols, between 0600hrs and 0900hrs, and thus they were once more allowed to make undisturbed attacks against the myriad of little ships moving to and fro off the beachhead.

The first attack commenced at 0720hrs when the first Ju87 appeared over the blazing town. The warships opened up with their pitifully few anti-aircraft guns and all boats got under way to take such avoiding action as they could.

First to be hit was the minesweeper *Skipjack* with 275 men aboard. She sank like a stone and very few of the troops got away. Next the destroyer *Keith*, which had Adm Wake-Walker aboard, was singled out for attack. She was down to her last 30 rounds of AA ammunition and there was little she could do except zig-zag violently to throw out the bombers' aim.

The first assault was made while she was under full port helm and no less than nine bombs exploded under her starboard side, throwing the racing ship right over on her beam ends and severely damaging her hull. Her rudder was jammed and she careered along in a tight circle. A second attack was then made on her and a heavy bomb went down her aft funnel and exploded in her boiler rooms, enveloping her in great clouds of steam. Near misses further damaged her and, listing 20 degrees to port and with less than two feet of freeboard, she came to a halt.

A tiny motor torpedo boat scurried up and took off the Admiral who re-hoisted his flag in another vessel. While this was happening, another destroyer, the *Basilisk*, was heavily hit aft by a bomb which killed eight men and wounded four. While trying to struggle back to Dover she had to be abandoned and 77 of her survivors were rescued by the French trawler *Jolie Mascotte*. The still-floating hulk of the *Basilisk* was found later by the *Whitehall* which sank it by torpedo. A third air raid took place on the *Keith* and the Stukas hit her yet again; she turned turtle and went down.

Two destroyers had gone and meanwhile others were also being savaged by the dive-bombers. The *Ivanhoe* was badly damaged and disabled and taken in tow by the tug *Persia*. The *Worcester* was damaged by bombs, involved in a collision and finally staggered back to Dover. The *Whitehall* was set on by Stukas, near-missed and damaged, and the little gunboat *Mosquito* was set ablaze by a direct hit, abandoned and sank later.

The brand new destroyer *Havant* came straight from the builder's yard and was thrown into the cauldron of Dunkirk. She was on her fourth trip to the beaches and had been embarking troops from the mole since 0730hrs. When the *Ivanhoe* was hit she went to her assistance and at 0900hrs *Havant* was proceeding down the channel laden with survivors when a heavy Stuka raid commenced Two bombs hit her engine-room and passed through her starboard side, while a third bomb landed 50yd ahead and exploded as she passed over it. An attempt was made at towing her by the minesweeper *Saltash*, but this failed and at 1015hrs, after further attacks, she rolled over and sank with the loss of 34 crew and soldiers.

A brief lull followed, but at 1300hrs the Ju87s were back over the beaches and further ships went down. The French destroyer *Foudroyant* was approaching the mole when 'she was submerged in a cloud of Stukas'. Hit by three bombs and deluged by near misses, she capsized instantly and went down.

Losses among the non-combatant ships also reached alarming proportions. The *Brighton Queen*, an ancient paddle-boat converted for minesweeping, had embarked 700 French troops and started out for Dover. A concentrated dive-bombing attack landed a 550lb bomb on her after-deck, decimating about half her passengers. The *Saltash* closed and took off the remainder before the old boat went down. The personnel vessel *Prague* was similarly laden with some 3,000 French troops when she was hit and damaged. The *Scotia* was sunk with 2,000 French soldiers aboard, many of whom lost their heads

amidst such slaughter and rushed the boats. The destroyer *Esk* closed on her and managed to take off the bulk of the survivors.

Eight Ju87s fell out of the sky upon a convoy of small French auxiliaries at 1600hrs, sinking the *Denis Papin* in 30 seconds and sinking the *Moussaillon* and *Venus* soon after. Despite suicidal patrols by Coastal Command and Fleet Air Arm units pretending to be fighters, fighter cover was not complete, although while it was there it was effective. The RAF claimed to have destroyed no less than 78 German aircraft in the vicinity that day, and Churchill later claimed this to be a 'victory within a deliverance'. In actual fact the Luftwaffe lost, all told, 29 aircraft – a dozen of these to ships' gunfire – while the British lost 31 aircraft. The evacuation fleet lost 31 ships sunk and 11 seriously damaged.

Hans-Joachim Lehmann was one of the original Stuka pilots who served throughout the Polish, French, Balkan, Crete and Russian campaigns, initially with 3/StG2 and latter as Geschwader TO in the Staff of StG2. He naturally has fond memories of the Ju87:

'I have followed the development of the Ju87 as a Technical Officer from the beginning right through all the various modifications to the end, and was, in the finish, in charge of the technical department with the General der Schlachtflieger. Through all these different activities I have, in the course of my flying career, flown 32 different types of aircraft, and therefore, I think I am allowed to have an opinion as to the performance of the various Luftwaffe types under combat conditions.

'I have thereby come to the conclusion that the Ju87 was probably the best type, overall, in the German Luftwaffe. Only the Ju52 could be classed equally as versatile and long-lasting. From a flying point of view it is established that all Junkers planes were excellent machines in both flying aspects and technical aspects. They were slow but, under certain circumstances, and especially in ground attack rôles, this could be an advantage.

'Over Dunkirk I was involved in a dog-fight for 15min, in close contact with an English Hawker Hurricane. The Hurricane couldn't get me simply because it was fast and, therefore, had too large a turning circle. With my Ju87 I could "turn on a plate", and therefore the Hurricane was never in a good enough position to shoot. I take my hat off to the English pilot, who tried ceaselessly but had to give in in the end so as to return to England with his remaining fuel.'

Such losses meant that the bulk of the remaining evacuation had to be made by night, for the Luftwaffe failed to operate after sunset, and although E-boats and U-boats were working off the approaches they were unable to do more than harry the convoys of rescue ships. Lack of targets for their bombers meant, for the Germans, the switching of operations, and before the Dunkirk evacuation had come to its remarkable conclusion the bulk of the Stuka forces were attacking French positions in readiness for the next thrust southward, the final campaign in the west.

There is no doubt that, for the British, the rescue of over 300,000 soldiers under the nose of the victorious Wehrmacht was a splendid victory in itself. It was all the more remarkable in view of the fact that the British themselves only expected to get 45,000 men away. The German admiral Schniewind said that it could not take place in the conditions prevailing and the French admiral, Darlan, had stated flatly to M. Reynaud: 'It will be impossible to carry out the evacuation.'

Rested and re-grouped, the whole combined land and air might of the German armed forces struck south on 5 June and broke through against weak French resistance that same day. Paris was taken on the 14th and three days later the French Government, ignoring Churchill's pleading cry of 'Common Citizenship', asked for terms. By 22 June, France had capitulated. On the actual effects that the 'Trombones of Jericho' had Waldemar Plewig provides a first-hand account:

'My wing was supplied with these so-called sirens. Trials with the "Organs" on the undercarriage of the Ju87 did not have the required success as they somersaulted when diving and made them useless. However my very clever works foreman, proposed fixing the ventilators with ball-bearings and this worked perfectly and by the start of the French campaign we were equipped with them. They were a big morale booster and I can give you two examples of this.

'At the training camp at Köln-Wahn just before 10 May 1940, we attacked a bunker. A large crowd of army Generals had come to watch. When the chain of Stukas attacked with their sirens in action it had a shocking affect on most of the onlookers. Never have I seen so many red trousers bending in front of one Leutnant and two sergeants, who were not so worried! Initially they had not been enthusiastic about the Stukas but after they saw the accuracy and effect they quickly changed their bias, and afterwards the army was only too glad of our constant support.

'During the actual campaign in France, one day while resting, we went out to look for an aircraft of ours which had crash landed and on the way we bumped into a group of French POW's who appeared to have no guards whatsoever with them. Our interpreter, Capt Psalter, asked where they were off to, and despite their unhappy situation one defiantly cried out "Berlin!", which tickled us. Then they asked us to which unit of aircraft we belonged and Psalter shouted back "Stukas". Immediately there was confusion and shouting in French up and down the line, "Attention Stukas" and in no time at all the whole column, they were part of an Infantry division, to the left and right of us were scrambling for cover in the roadside ditches. It was not easy to persuade the confused "Poilus" to get up again, they were still awaiting the oncoming planes! Their actions proved the effect of the sirens.'

For the British units caught up in this débâcle the story of retreat was repeated and the British destroyer flotillas were again flung in to pull the troops to safety, although they themselves were still battered and reeling from continuous operations and heavy losses. The scene shifted down to the great French harbours of Le Havre, Cherbourg, Brest, St Nazaire and La Pallice. The locations varied, but the story was much the same: exhausted troops fighting desperate rearguard actions, falling back to the sea where the Royal Navy was waiting for them.

The Luftwaffe was active on a reduced scale over all the embarkation points and losses among the ships were again severe. On 11 June the personnel ship *Bruges* was hit and sunk off Dieppe and the *Bulldog* was hit and damaged by Stukas on the previous day. This destroyer managed to struggle back to Portsmouth, but by far the greatest loss was the liner *Lancastria* which was bombed and sunk off St Nazaire with the loss of over 3,000 troops. Nevertheless a total of 191,000 troops were brought safely back to England, across far greater stretches of water than at Dunkirk.

With the Armistice signed, the Germans controlled the whole Atlantic coastline from the tip of Norway down to the Spanish frontier. The English Channel was now the front-line, and the British Isles were besieged. The triumphant German forces now awaited the signal to begin the invasion of Britain but first there was a lull. Hitler had hoped that the British would now initiate peace terms without the necessity of such an invasion, which was liable to prove costly to him; indeed, he openly proposed such a course. Failing that he would invade, but only once the Royal Air Force had been smashed and the Royal Navy cleared from the path of his invasion fleet. It was to the completion of these objectives that the Luftwaffe now turned their attention.

4 Closing the Channel

While much of the Luftwaffe took the opportunity to refit and rest, and while Hitler awaited the British reply to his Peace speech, the Kommadore of KG2, Johannes Fink, received special instructions at the beginning of July to set up a new anti-shipping striking force along the Channel coast. His mission was to close the Straits of Dover to all English shipping, to drive the Royal Navy's fast destroyer forces from the area between Portsmouth and Dover, and to gain and hold air superiority over the coastal waters preparatory to the launching of an invasion should it prove to be necessary after all.

Cooperating with the Kanalkampffuehrer, whose headquarters were set up in a converted omnibus on the cliff top at Cap Blanc overlooking the battleground, were the Stukas of von Richthofen's Fliegerkorps VIII based between Cherbourg and Dieppe. It was to be a strictly limited offensive, which, once its objectives were achieved, would be followed by the destruction of the fighter defences of southern England, which would be achieved by the launching of 'Adlertag' (Eagle Day). On the completion of both these tasks, the maintenance of air and sea superiority in the English Channel; the invasion would follow. Goering was supremely confident that his Luftwaffe could manage both tasks, other Germans were not so sure.

Fink and Richthofen had numerous Stuka units to aid them in their task, and during July and August there were fought a series of ever increasingly fierce battles between the dive-bombers on one hand and the destroyers and coastal convoys on the other, with skirmishing between the opposing fighter forces.

On 2 July Stuka forces were distributed as follows:

II Fliegerkorps – Bruno Loerzer – Pas de Calais.
II/StG1 and IV(Stuka)/LG1.
VIII Fliegerkorps – Wolfram von Richthofen. StG77 – Flers. StG2 – Falaise. StG1 – Cherbourg.
7/StG51 operated with VIII Fliegerkorps for a time before being reformed as 4/StG1,

and later in the battle StG3 moved up in support.

On the second day of the campaign the Stukas made a notable contribution in clearing the Channel of ships. An Atlantic convoy, OA168, had penetrated the Straits on its way out and had been located by German patrols off Portland. The RAF had informed the Admiralty the day before that Fighter Command's duty was the defence of the United Kingdom and not the protection of shipping, but such an easy dismissal of its responsibilities was not to survive the day's Stuka assault.

The whole stregth of StG2, 90 dive-bombers was deployed against this unhappy convoy, which was protected only by the ship's guns, and the results were devastating. While two Gruppen struck the convoy itself in a textbook attack, the third peeled off over Portland itself inflicting considerable damage.

Four large ships of the convoy were sunk, totalling 16,000 tons, and a further nine were hit and damaged, some badly, which amounted to a further 40,000 tons. Two more ships were hit in Portland harbour and the only loss suffered by StG2 was one Ju87B brought down by anti-aircraft fire. Nor was the convoy completely defenceless, for included in its escort was the auxiliary anti-aircraft ship, *Foylebank*.

This vessel, although only a converted merchant ship, had the AA firepower of a cruiser, with eight 4in guns mounted in twin turrets, two quadruple pom-poms and four of the new 20mm Oerlikons. Her equipment was extensive, with air and sea warning radar sets and gunnery directors. She was no sitting duck, therefore, but Richthofen's Stukas had little trouble despatching her in Portland harbour.

The shock of this defeat caused serious repercussions throughout the Admiralty and Air Ministry. Churchill, in a strong note, ordered Dowding that in future all convoys were to be provided with a six-plane escort during their entire passage through the Channel. The Navy, aghast at such heavy losses on its doorstep, stopped all further

Atlantic convoys from passing through the Straits and routed them north-about. Henceforth only small local convoys were to be risked in the 'English' Channel.

To provoke the RAF into using up its precious fighter force, Fink sent out small Stuka forces over Portsmouth and Spithead on the 7th, with heavy fighter protection; but Dowding refused to be drawn. Unable to find more worthwhile targets, the dive-bombers blasted a coastal gun battery on the Isle of Wight. On the 9th they sank the coaster *Kenneth Hawksfield* off Sandwich.

On 11 July the Stukas had little better fortune. Although a force of 10 Ju87Bs located a convoy off Portland at 0700hrs that morning and delivered an attack, they had to evade intercepting Hurricanes and no ships of the convoy were sunk. They did send to the bottom the ancient armed yacht *Warrior II*, a vessel of the Inner Patrol against invasion. Other small raids resulted in the loss of two aircraft.

Poor weather in the battle zone resulted in the scaling down of air activity, although the Ju87s were active whenever possible. IV(Stuka)/LG1 directed a heavy attack by three Staffeln against a convoy off Dover during the afternoon of the 14th damaging the coasters *Betswood* and *Bovey Tracey*. Five days later, a similar raid was mounted in the same area and the dive-bombers attacked Dover harbour itself which was being used as an anti-invasion base by the 4th Destroyer Flotilla.

By far the biggest raid of this quiet period took place on the 20th when convoy 'Bossum' was found scurrying through the Straits some 10 miles off Dover. Two of the 4th Flotilla's destroyers provided their escort, the *Brazen* and the *Beagle*.

Opposing them was II/StG1 led by Hauptmann Keil. His unit dived out of the sky at 1738hrs and hit the convoy just as the defending fighters from No 32 Squadron made contact. However, the British fighters were soon diverted by the Bf109s and 110s of the Stukas' escort, and the dive-bombers were able to continue their attacks, sinking the collier *Pulborough I* and damaging another. Other Stukas went for the destroyer escort and the *Beagle* was slightly damaged by bomb splinters from a near-miss. Not so fortunate was the *Brazen*; she received hits which so crippled her that she sank in tow the following day, and, although she claimed the destruction of three dive-bombers, Keil's unit lost no aircraft in this raid.

The loss of this destroyer was a serious blow, for the Navy's front-line defence against the expected invasion fleet relied heavily on fast destroyer forces whose high speed would, it was hoped, make them more immune from air

Above left: Wireless operator's view of Stuka in a dive. /*Archiv Schliephake*

Left: A Stuka in full cry. /*Ullstein*

Above : A Staffel commander inspects his unit. /*Ullstein*

Above right: Clip from a film showing three Stukas en echelon./*IWM*

attack than other naval units. The C-in-C Home Fleet was reluctant to station heavy units in the south so close to German bomber bases, but no less than 36 destroyers were on hand at bases like Harwich, Sheerness and Dover. If the Stukas could drive these warships out of the Channel there was little hope for the diverse smaller and slower units hurriedly formed for anti-invasion rôles.

Dover, less than nine minutes' flying time across the Channel, was particularly vulnerable, and the 4th Flotilla was in the front-line. A typical destroyer force of the period, it had originally consisted of eight fairly modern ships of 1,400 tons displacement armed with four 4·7in low-angled guns and torpedo tubes, with a slightly larger flotilla leader, the *Keith*. However, the British destroyers of this type were ill-equipped to fight off any determined dive-bombing.

The flotilla had been reduced to eight ships by May 1940, and, as we have seen, had already suffered heavily at the hands of the Ju87. *Keith* and *Basilisk* were sunk by them at Dunkirk on 1 June, *Bulldog* was damaged on the 10th and the *Boadicea* was put out of action by an aircraft torpedo off Portland on the 13th. With the loss of the *Brazen* the flotilla was down to three units and these were not long to survive their sisters.

Clear weather over the Channel and the persistency of the British in sailing further convoys led to a rapid escalation of the combats in the narrow waters towards the end of July. A large convoy, CW8, attempted to force the passage on the morning of the 25th. Originaly there were 21 coasters escorted by two armed trawlers and they were off Deal by the late afternoon. Fink's command post had patiently

watched the smoky little squadron crawl through the Downs all day and now it unleashed the dive-bombers to obliterate them.

In all 57 Stukas in three waves and heavily escorted by fighters struck the convoy which soon became dispersed. The first attack was mounted by III/StG51 which hit and sank two coasters, *Ajax* and *Coquetdale*, damaged another, *Empire Crusader*, and set ablaze a small tanker which burned for 24 hours. Further attacks mounted by II/StG1 sank the cement carrier *Summity* and the collier *Henry Moon*. Defending fighters from No 54 Squadron became heavily embroiled with the escorting German fighters and the Stukas lost only two bombers, off Dover.

With the convoy a mass of burning and sinking vessels, the Germans felt secure enough to send out an E-boat squadron in broad daylight to complete the destruction, but in this they were imprudent. No match for the Ju87s, the Royal Navy was still quite capable of dealing with any surface threat, and the destroyers *Brilliant* and *Boreas* at once put out from Dover and engaged them. The E-boats laid smoke and hurriedly retreated from the scene, but not before several of them received hits and damage. But in the zeal to hit the enemy the two destroyers got carried away with the thrill of the chase and followed the enemy almost into Calais, which was somewhat rash.

Fink despatched further formations of Ju87s to deal with them; he was quite indignant about the fact that 'two little boats' had intruded into his operation. Twenty-four Stukas caught the destroyers some three miles off Dover and inflicted severe damage on them. The *Boreas* took two bombs through her

Right: Ju87B2s of II/StG77 with their cockerel emblem. /*Wolfinger via Archiv Schliephake*

Below: 3/StG2 with their distinctive 'Scottie' emblem. /*Archiv Schliephake*

Bottom: A stepped up echelon formation of Stukas in the usual position preparatory to the wing-over attack./*IWM*

bridge structure which killed and wounded 50 men, while the *Brilliant* was twice hit aft. The bombs pierced her quarterdeck but luckily failed to explode. Both ships made it back to harbour but this was almost the last participation by the 4th Flotilla in the Channel battle.

Out of 21 ships which had comprised CW8, five were sunk and six damaged in the space of a few hours and a later E-boat attack sank a further three. It was enough. For the time being the Admiralty acknowledged the Stuka's dominance and all convoys were prevented from using the Channel in the Dover area.

With the convoys halted, Fink and Richthofen turned their attentions to what remained of the destroyer forces in the area. On the 27th another small convoy, 'Bacon' was attacked by I/StG77 off Swanage, but the main attentions of the Luftwaffe were concentrated against the warships. Ju88s hit Dover harbour and sank the flotilla leader *Codrington* outside and smashed up the destroyer *Walpole*, which was lying alongside the depot ship *Sandhurst* inside. The wreck was towed away to Chatham out of danger. At the same time Heinkels operating against a convoy off the Suffolk coast sank the destroyer *Wren* and damaged the *Montrose*.

Dover was finally abandoned as a forward base after another severe raid on the 29th, when 48 Ju87s, six Staffeln drawn from IV(Stuka)/LG1 and II/StG1, all escorted by 80 Bf109s, dive-bombed the harbour and sank the patrol ship *Gulzar*. On the same day a low level attack sank the destroyer *Delight* off Portland, with one direct hit and a near-miss. Stuka losses for the day amounted to four.

On this date the Admiralty prohibited all use of destroyers in the Channel by day, even although some senior officers still thought that destroyers, steaming at full speed and with full manoeuvring power, should be fairly immune. This would apply to resisting an invasion fleet but for convoy escort something else had to be tried.

There now followed a break in the fighting. The Germans had, by their own success, brought about a lack of targets and in any case they were now fully engaged in preparing for the next phase of their plan, which involved the extension of the raids from shipping to ports, radar installations and defence works on the south coast. Meanwhile the British made changes in the defensive structure of coastal shipping. They knew that the continued sailings were essential but now they decided that the most dangerous part of the passage, the Straits, would have to be forced by night.

Other measures were taken: kite balloons were to be flown from ships, a Channel guard of volunteer AA gunners was formed to sail with each convoy, more powerful fighter cover was to be provided and the new Hunt class destroyers, the first of which were now entering service, with mainly anti-aircraft armaments, took up the duty of escort.

At first these new measures appeared to be the answer, for the first convoy to adopt them, CE8, passed through from Folkstone to the Thames without hindrance. Unknown to the British, however, Fink had at his disposal a surface radar set, the Freya system, which had a range of 75 miles. On this every move of the 'hidden' convoy was watched and plotted. When the reciprocal west-bound convoy left the assembly point off Southend on the evening of 7 August, Fink was ready.

CW9 passed Dover that night and found the E-boats in position waiting for it. They sank three ships and damaged two, and by dawn the convoy had lost all semblance of order. It was further scattered after a small group of Ju87s harried it during the forenoon. From Portsmouth the destroyers *Bulldog* and *Fernie* sailed to render assistance and help the little ships reform, but before they could do so Fink sent in what he hoped would be his big punch.

The morning attacks had been mounted by StG1 which lost two bombers in the process. The second wave caught the convoy off the Isle of Wight. Fifty-seven Stukas from various formations arrived overhead but were met by strong fighter defences which caused them serious losses. It was the first time that the RAF with its eight-gun fighters, Hurricanes and Spitfires, had really got in among the slow-flying Ju87s, and the results of the one-sided contest were plain.

I/StG3 lost three planes and had another damaged, while I/StG2 and III/StG2 each had one bomber shot up. 2/StG77, which attacked in the third wave, was decimated, losing three bombers with a further five damaged. When 82 Stukas of Richthofen's units attacked further ships in Weymouth Bay, they too met strong opposition. Even so it was insufficient to prevent the slaughter of CW9. Four merchantmen were sunk and six badly damaged, and six small rescue ships which put out to aid them were also set upon by dive-bombers and wrecked. The enemy's losses were the heaviest so far, eight Ju87s being destroyed.

It was during these heavy attacks on the 'Peewit' convoy on 8 August that the Kommandeur of II/StG77, Waldemar Plewig, was shot down. His unit, codenamed 'Puma', as we have seen, suffered the most heavy losses this day. A graphic account of this mission was written by one of his fellow flyers:

'To find the convoy was difficult for we had no proper up-to-date location, and so we had to fly as accurately as we could by compass. The formation leader had to give his various unit commanders the most brief and accurate instructions possible. Then everyone prepared. The most important piece of clothing on this mission is the life-jacket. Shortly before 1600hrs the whole squadron was ready, the first formation into the air was our Kommandeur's. A small signal and, like a flock of large birds, the whole force rose up, one after another, into the air. We all collect together, then set off towards the Channel.

'After only a few minutes we are at the coast. Below us, as far as the eye can see, is the Channel. Once it was the greatest shipping lane, now it is the biggest ships' graveyard.

'Water – nothing but water below us, we can no longer see the coast, or any ships. Our thoughts are with our engines, those reliable, humming helpers in our operation. Our eyes go from instrument to instrument checking, water cooling, tachometer, pressure gauge, all are constantly checked, if our engines give up there is only one thing for us and that is: *Wasser*! The English Channel is wide and large and on the other side is the "Island".

'And there it is, carefully, one would almost say, shy, from the blue-green water emerges a light strip, at first you can hardly see it. The English south coast, the white cliffs of the steep shoreline. A few hundred metres above us fly some squadrons of fighters and long-range fighters as protection for us. Half-right, in front of us, at about a height of 3,000–4,000m, the first air battle has already begun. You can hardly tell friend from enemy. We can only see small silver spots curving in the sky. Now it means we must be specially alert. The coast is coming nearer, to the left, below us, the Isle of Wight, and there we can also now see 10 or 12 ships, the convoy. They, as they sight us, start to take avoiding action by zig-zagging their lines. We fly steadily onwards from the east. Suddenly we hear through the W/T; ". . . No 4 aircraft has crash landed." An Unteroffizier from our 4th Staffel has had to go down in the sea. His engine must have failed. We hope he makes it alright.

' "Puma One to all Pumas. Attack". We are above the convoy, it seems to be all small ships. The first squadron has already started its attack. Now the formations pull apart and split up. Each one of them chooses a ship that has so far not been hit by other squadrons. The Kommandeurs' own formation starts to dive closer to the coast; but what's this? *Four* aircraft? I can't believe my eyes, and then, also by the 3rd Kette, which is attacking to our left, the same picture. At the same instant I hear, "Puma alert, enemy fighter diving from above." When thus diving and banking the English hardly have a chance to shoot accurately at our planes, and on account of them being so much faster they had to intercept sooner than they would have wished thus giving our pilots still time to aim. I attack with my Kette the most southerly ship of the convoy. Before I commence my dive I make sure by asking my radio operator if everything is clear behind me. "All clear, Herr Oberleutnant". Then we go into our attack dive, without braking, in the present tense situation it is imperative we all close up again quickly. My bombs land close alongside the ship, while my Kettenhund flyer on my left also misses it by a very small margin, but the third one of our Kette hits the ship directly amidships. In a matter of seconds a large flame shoots up from the target, a big cloud of smoke follows from inside it, and as we fly away we can see the ship listing badly.

'Now the English are right on top of us. Spitfires, Hurricanes. From a distance you can't distinguish them from our own Bf109s. Above the Isle of Wight is developing a terrible air battle. About 60 aircraft of all types, German and English, fighting for their lives. Some of the English fighters draw back towards the mainland coast, while on the left of me a Bf109 drops into the sea, the pilot is able to get out and slowly he glides with his parachute towards the water. Another aircraft, the identity of which I cannot ascertain, circles in flames like a bonfire above us, explodes and falls down in small pieces. You can only recognise the tailplane.

'When we have reassembled toward the south the English again take us on. Only weaving helps if you want to escape the eight machine guns of the English fighters. The Radio Operators shoot whenever their guns

will bear. Again and again the English attack from astern. Again and again I hear the bullets striking my aircraft, but I don't think my engine has been hit, the motor is quiet and smooth. The closer we get to the middle of the Channel, the fewer English attack us. The various units find each other and close up, bit by bit. To the left of us flies the 4th Staffel. One of its aircraft has a long smoke trail behind it. The pilot gives us a brief message. "Aircraft damaged, going into the water." At that instant a Spitfire appears from ahead, firing, and hits him and down into the sea the plane goes. But the Englishman does not enjoy his glory for very long, for as he veers away he in turn is hit by a Bf109 and dives vertically into the water.

'After 30 minutes flying we at last see the coast of Normandy. We all sigh with relief. My Kettenhunde comrades close up to my aircraft, nod and smile. Everything in our Staffel appears to be alright. We land at our station. Unbelievably all the aircraft from our Staffel have returned. Some of them have up to 40 bullet holes in their fuselages and wings, but all managed to land alright. After about an hour the Kommandant comes back from reporting, very serious. "The Kommandant of the mission is missing, as are two others of his unit." We can't believe it. No one saw the Kommandant ditch. After the attack we saw him with the Stab formation. A few weeks later we found out that he was a prisoner of war in England, he had to ditch the plane which most likely had been hit, and was captured.'

Above: Target briefing. In close support operations of the precise nature assigned to Stuka units, up-to-date details of friendly and enemy units was essential. Here a Gruppen commander goes over a mission one last time before the sortie./*Lehmann*

In fact Plewig's plane was hit by a Hurricane of No 145 Squadron and he spent the rest of the war in captivity. He was awarded the Knights Cross which had been sent to England and it was awarded to him by the commander of the POW camp with full honours. He was also later promoted to Major on 1 April 1942.

Adolf Galland was operating with JG26, flying fighter escort to the Stuka Gruppen at this time, and he described the difficulties involved:

'Here the slow speed of the Ju87 turned out to be a great drawback. Owing to the speed-reducing effect of the externally-suspended bomb load, she only reached 150mph when diving, and as the required altitude for the dive was between 10,000 and 15,000ft, these Stukas attracted the Spitfires and the Hurricanes as honey attracts flies. The necessary fighter protection for such sorties was considerable and the task of the pilots fraught with difficulties. The British soon found that the Stukas, once they peeled out of formation to dive singly on to their target, were practically defenceless until they had reassembled. We made numerous attempts to counteract this shortcoming. With our greater speed, it was impossible to follow the Stukas into the dive without dive-brakes; equally impossible was the idea of providing fighter cover on all different levels between the start of the dive and the pull-out.'*

*Adolf Galland; *The First and the Last*; Methuen, London.

In fact the period of the dive was equally impossible for the attacking fighters, for the same problems applied to them; it was after they had pulled out and sought to reform where the real danger lay, but this was not apparently appreciated by Galland. Nevertheless, Stuka losses had not yet reached alarming proportions and the results of their attacks were impressive. In the Official History of the *War at Sea*, the effects are summed up: 'The seriousness of the enemy's effort lay in the fact that, at their peak, one ship in three in these convoys had been damaged or sunk. Such unattractive odds could, if continued, make it impossible to man the ships.'

Fortunately for the Navy it was now that Goering decided that the time had come to move on to the next phase of the plan, time in fact to launch the long-cherished Eagle Day. Therefore, commencing on 13 August, Stuka targets were gradually shifted away from the battered convoys to airfields and radar stations. The little ships were reprieved.

The last assault on a convoy at this time took place on 12 August when 22 Ju87s from

IV(Stuka)/LG1, commanded by Hauptmann von Brauchitsch, struck at shipping in the Thames Estuary, hitting two vessels. By the end of this phase the British had lost some 24,000 tons of shipping.

'Adlertag' opened at 0740hrs on 13 August but the Stuka Gruppen were not committed until the late afternoon. Fifty-two Ju87s of StG77 were sent to attack convoys and installations off Portland. Fortunately for the ships the weather was bad over the target area and the attack was a flop. Worse, from the German viewpoint, was the fact that the Stukas were intercepted by 15 Spitfires of No 609 Squadron which shot down five of them. A 10% loss rate on the first mission boded ill for the dive-bomber forces.

Better luck attended the aircraft of IV(Stuka)/LG1. Their target was the Coastal Command airfield of Detling, which was the base of Anson bombers of No 500 Squadron. The Stukas, 40 strong, arrived over the target at 1715hrs and carried out a classic attack. The whole airfield was flattened and 22 bombers ,together with hangars and workshops, were destroyed without loss of a single Ju87.

Another raid was made by StG2 against Rochford airfield but was 'weathered out'. Forty-six Stukas took part, but none were able to bomb and returned to base.

On the 15th the pace quickened and at noon II/StG1, commanded by Hauptmann Kiel, and IV(Stuka)/LG1 combined to hit the airfields at Lympne and Hawkinge. Again devastation was great and Lympne was completely out of action for two days. Other strikes made included 40 Ju87s of Hauptmann Hozzel's I/StG1 and Hauptmann Enneccerus's II/StG2 against targets in the Portland area. These were feints designed to draw away the British fighters towards the west but the bait was not taken and the Germans suffered no losses.

Airfields so singled out for destruction on the afternoon of the 16th included Tangmere. StG2 hit installations and the command post and caused severe damage but losses were heavy, nine Stukas being brought down in this attack and three more badly damaged. Losses of this scale were obviously prohibitive, although 14 British bombers were destroyed on the ground in these attacks.

Five Stukas bombed Ventnor radar station, dropping 22 bombs on the target and effectively putting it out of action, and other targets for the dive-bombers included Gosport Naval Air Station. At the same time Ju88s screamed down on Lee-on-Solent. At Gosport both main hangars were struck and burned for the rest of the day. Incredibly the Stukas found the naval aircraft lined up in neat rows on the runways as if there was no war on at all.

Presented with such a target at this stage of the war they could hardly fail to miss, and the wreckage of Albacores, Skuas and Rocs littered the runways after they had taken their departure minutes later.

There was a lull on the 17th, but the next day saw the Stukas back in force. It was to prove their last fling, for on that day the Ju87 was to suffer the severest casualties ever. Richthofen despatched four Stukagruppen against Gosport, Thorney Island and Ford airfields while others struck at Poling radar station.

The first unit to arrive over the target area was I/StG77 comprising 28 Stukas led by Hauptmann Meisel. They hit Poling as planned and caused extensive damage, but on pulling out of their dives they were caught by Spitfires and Hurricanes of No 152 and 43 Squadrons before they had time to reform and were decimated. Twelve Stukas were shot down, including Meisel's, and a further six damaged. II and III/StG77, 27 and 30 aircraft respectively, bombed Thorney Island and Ford with effect but also suffered heavily in the process. Altogether StG77 lost 14 Ju87s in this one raid and had eight more damaged – 20% losses. There was no alternative, the Stuka units were pulled out of the battle and concentrated in the Calais area.

Here they would be on hand to support the Army in the traditional manner should air superiority be won. It was left to the faster medium bombers, Do17s, He111s and Ju88s, to wrest that control. Without it the Stuka could not operate, but as they failed, so the heavier bombers also failed. Attacks continued through into October without a decisive result and already Hitler was planning his Eastern campaign.

The Stuka units were gradually withdrawn to prepare for other operations, but during November it was decided to once again revert to anti-shipping strikes. The results were promising to start with. On 1 November 5/StG1 attacked ships in the Thames Estuary off Margate and further raids were made on the 8th by 3/StG3 and 11th by 9/StG1 against convoys in the same area which achieved a total of seven merchant ship casualties.

But on the 14th the British concentrated large numbers of fighters in readiness for such a repeat operation and Hauptmann Mahlke's III/StG1 was intercepted by them. Despite the fact that two whole fighter Geschwader were assigned to protect the dive-bombers, all the German fighter escorts missed the rendezvous in poor weather and the Gruppe lost a quarter of its strength. This was the final blow, and the onset of winter conditions off the English coast meant the ending of any further raids by Stukas against Britain.

5 Début in the Mediterranean

'On 19 August', records one official Air Ministry Pamphlet, 'Fliegerkorps VIII, which possessed 220 of the total of 280 Ju87s engaged was withdrawn from the Cherbourg area and put under the control of Luftflotte 2 in the Pas de Calais area. This move, besides pointing to the realisation by the Germans that the dive-bomber had been a failure in attacks on shipping, was in effect a new disposal of forces in preparation for the invasion itself.'*

To say that the Stuka had proved itself a failure in attacks on shipping was a misleading statement, for the Ju87 had shown itself to be just about the only bomber on either side capable of hitting shipping at all. What the move did confirm was that when put up against the main force of RAF Fighter Command the Stuka was simply annihilated without strong air cover. That is all it did prove, and the fact that subsequently the faster medium bombers of the Luftwaffe met exactly the same fate, has been overlooked in this summary writing off by the RAF of the Stuka.

Repulsed by the strong defences over southern England, the Ju87 groups still had a major rôle to play, but with the abandonment

*The Rise and Fall of the German Air Force; Pamphlet 248 (1948).

of Operation Sealion their future deployment initially lay to the south, over the sunny waters of the Mediterranean Sea.

Here the Royal Navy had been supreme for over a century, and events in the second half of 1940 only served to prove that the new navy of Italy could in no way dispute that fact. Since the Italian declaration of war the Mediterranean had been the centre of naval activity and a series of resounding victories had been chalked up by the navy there which did much to lift the flagging spirits in besieged Britain.

The surface actions of Calabria in July and Spartivento in November plus the numerous smaller actions, all had the same result, the defeat of or the flight of the Italian Fleet. Nor had attempts by the numerically large Regia Aeronautica done anything to redress the balance of power. Committed as it largely was to the high altitude bomber, its massed assaults caused only a few minor damage casualties to the British fleets. More dangerous was its torpedo-bomber unit, the Aerosiluranti, but at this period this was only a minor arm of the Italian Air Force.

The standard of bombing by the Italians was very high and time and time again massed assaults were made on the ships and convoys. A Fleet Air Arm pilot who served aboard *Ark Royal* recalled:

Below: One of the first Stukas to arrive in Sicily in 1940 is the subject of great interest. /AMI via N. Malizia

57

'They would always come over at the same altitude in perfect formation. Despite our attacks they would hold on for the fleet and their commander would order "bombs away" and when one looked down at the fleet all one could see were bomb bursts, and one would think, Goodbye *Ark* and now where do I land? But after a short while a destroyer would poke its nose out of the spray and smoke, and then another and another until finally the battleships and the *Ark* would emerge unscathed and nonchalant.'*

It says nothing to detract from the bravery of the Italian pilots of the SM79s to state that in the period June–December 1940 they proved to everyone's satisfaction that high-level bombing of ships at sea was at best a very poor return for a great deal of effort. The Italians certainly realised this themselves and over the next two years most of their bomber Gruppi changed over to torpedo-bomber conversions of the SM79 while others were re-equipped with the Ju87 supplied by Germany and renamed the *Picchiatello*.

As if to add the final seal of the Royal Navy's dominance of Mare Nostrum, the aircraft carrier *Illustrious* arrived to reinforce Adm Cunningham's fleet. She was the first of the new carriers under construction for the Royal Navy, larger than the *Ark Royal*, and she had one added refinement that was to prove a godsend, an armoured flight-deck, the first of its kind. Three inches thick, it was designed to withstand the impact of 500lb bombs, the largest then envisaged. The idea was a revolutionary one and one which the other

*Recorded Interview with Cdr R. C. Hay, 1969.

major naval powers scorned, for it cut down the number of combat aircraft which could be carried.

Illustrious was not slow in proving her worth and in November she sent her obsolete Swordfish torpedo-bombers against the Italian fleet berthed behind nets and barrage balloons at Taranto, sinking three of the six battleships of the Duce's fleet.

To Hitler, this humiliation of his partner coupled with the defeats the Italian armies were suffering in the attempted invasion of Greece, proved the last straw. Although engrossed with his plan to settle accounts with the hated Soviet Russia, Operation Barbarossa he ordered a small armoured unit, the Afrika Korps, to Libya to bolster the flagging Italian armies there. More important, in order to wrest control of the Central Mediterranean from the Royal Navy so that he could keep his land force supplied, he sent Gen der Flieger Geisler with his anti-shipping command Fliegerkorps X from Norway down to Sicily. With them came, as chief of staff, Oberst Harlinghausen, the ship-busting expert (his ideas finally being listened to), and the Stukas. Their prime objective was flatly stated: 'Sink the *Illustrious*'.

With the effective status of a Luftflotte and operating directly under the orders of the German Air Ministry in Berlin, Fliegerkorps X comprised 120 medium bombers, 40 single-engined fighters, 20 reconnaissance machines and, as the tip of the spear, 150 Stukas.

Harlinghausen and Geisler had studied the effects of the dive-bombing attacks carried out against warships and they estimated that given the same scale of resistance the Ju87s could sink a ship of the *Illustrious* type, armour deck or no, with four direct hits. No warship

had yet been hit so hard, but it should be well within the capacity of the Stukas to hit the great flat-top target offered by the carrier's flight-deck, it was thought. The pilots of StG2 were now given intensive training to perfect the necessary tactics to carry out this one operation using a floating mock-up of a carrier. They soon proved that the necessary four hits were by no means impossible and settled down to await their opportunity.

In January, just as the German pilots had completed their training, the navy granted them their wish: a complex series of convoy operations was put in hand to reinforce Malta, Operation Excess. The plan was for a convoy of five merchant ships, *Essex* for Malta, *Clan Cummings*, *Clan Macdonald* and *Empire Song* for Alexandria to sail from Gibralter on the evening of the 6th escorted by Force H, *Renown*, *Malaya*, *Ark Royal* and destroyers. Accompanying this force would be the cruiser *Bonaventure* and further destroyers intended as reinforcements for Adm Cunningham's fleet.

The merchant ships were to be met in the Sicilian straits by detachments of the Mediterranean Fleet – *Warspite*, *Valiant*, *Illustrious* and eight destroyers, reinforced by the cruisers *Gloucester* and *Southampton* and two destroyers and the cruiser *Sydney* and destroyer *Stuart* from Malta. Numerous subsidiary operations were in train at the same time, including the passage of four corvettes and an oiler from west to east, an air attack on the Dodecanese Islands by *Eagle*, *Barham* and five destroyers, and troop convoys in the Aegean.

All this complex movement took place without incident until dawn on the 10th when the complicated handover procedure of the convoy

Above: Among the first Stukas assigned to the Regia Aeronautica, this is one of the aircraft of 96° Gruppo Bombardamento a Tuffo, at Comiso airfield in 1940. /*G. Fiorin via N. Malizia*

Left: The emblem of 102° Gruppo Tuffatori of 5° Stormo. /*AMI via N. Malizia*

Below left: The emblem of 96° Gruppo Tuffatori on the undercarriage of the aircraft. /*AMI via N. Malizia*

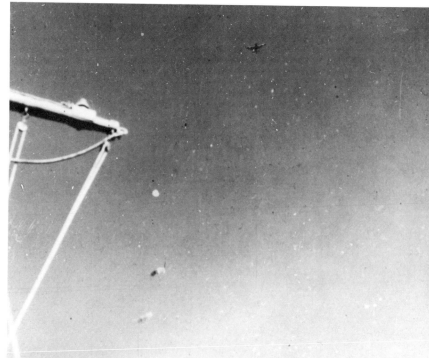

got under way in the Narrows less than an hour's flight from Comiso and Catania where lay the patient aircraft of StG2 fully bombed-up and ready to go. The fleet had been reported and shadowed since 1030hrs the previous day and it allowed the ships to steam farther into the trap.

Just after dawn two Italian destroyers blundered into the path of the now-joined cruiser force and the *Southampton* and *Bonaventure* with the destroyers *Jaguar* and *Hereward* hotly engaged them, blowing the *Vega* to pieces and chasing the other as she fled at high speed to the north-west. Adm Cunningham steered to close the scene of the action. At 0815hrs contact was made with the convoy and a fighter patrol of five Fulmars was flown off to patrol over it. Force H had meantime turned back to the west and took no further part in the battle.

At 0834hrs the destroyer *Gallant* was torpedoed and damaged and the *Mohawk* took her in tow. The 3rd Cruiser Squadron, *Southampton*, *Gloucester* and *Bonaventure*, were detached to stand by her. The *Bonaventure* was a brand-new anti-aircraft cruiser of the Dido class whose 5·25in guns were to prove one of the best AA weapons to be adopted by the fleet, and her departure from Cunningham's screen was to be sorely regretted before the day was out.

At 0834hrs the *Gallant* was hit but it was not until 1223hrs that the first attack took place. The Germans knew all about those five Fulmars and between 1223hrs and 1229hrs Italian SM79 torpedo-bombers were sent in low over the sea to make a determined attack on the *Valiant*. The battleship avoided the

torpedoes launched at her and they passed astern. Two of the Fulmars came down after the Italian aircraft but the SM79s had the speed, and putting their noses down they lured the fighters away from them. The other three Fulmars were also ineffective, two had expended all their ammunition on previous enemy feints and one had been damaged. The fleet was therefore without airborne defence, and another six Fulmars, all that remained, were prepared by *Illustrious* to take their place.

At 1230hrs the radar screens picked up a large formation of enemy aircraft approaching from the north. Capt Boyd of the *Illustrious* at once recalled the two airborne Fulmars and asked for permission to turn into the wind to fly off the others, but before this could be effected the Germans were on them.

There were 43 Stukas; II/StG2 led by Maj Enneccerus and I/StG1 commanded by Hauptmann Hozzel, and they made no mistakes. They approached from 12,000ft and then split up into clover-leaf formation, constantly varying their heights as they selected their targets. One unit of 10 aircraft peeled off and dived on the battleships. With the anti-aircraft fire of the most powerful vessels thus fully engaged the other Stukas turned their fury on the main target, the carrier.

Adm Cunningham recalled:

'One was too interested in this new form of dive-bombing attack to be frightened, and there was no doubt that we were watching complete experts. Formed roughly in a large circle over the fleet they peeled off one by one when reaching the attacking position. We

Above left: Maj Walter Enneccerus led II/StG2 in the successful attacks on the aircraft carriers *Illustrious* and *Formidable* and in the sinking of the cruiser *Southampton*, all in the Mediterranean during 1941. /*Ullstein*

Above: The ordeal of the *Illustrious*. A Stuka claws up into the clear blue sky dotted with white flak bursts (centre top) after delivering her payload into the heart of the stricken vessel./*IWM*

Above right: The ordeal of *Illustrious*. The Royal Navy's long-established dominance of the Mediterranean, enhanced by numerous victories over the Italian Fleet in 1940, received a severe set-back when the Stukas of Fliegerkorps X cornered the carrier *Illustrious* off Malta on 10 January 1941. Here the ship is immersed in the smoke and spray of near misses and direct hits./*IWM*

Right: The ordeal of *Illustrious*. The Stuka's 1,000kg armour-piercing bombs penetrated even the carrier's armoured flight deck and punched their way into her innards./*IWM*

could not but admire the skill and precision of it all. The attacks were pressed home to point-blank range, and as they pulled out of their dives some were seen to fly along the flightdeck of the *Illustrious* below the level of the funnel.'*

The attack lasted for only six and a half minutes but in that time the Ju87s created absolute devastation aboard the carrier. Dives were made from 12,000–7,000ft and heights of bomb release varied from between 1,200–800ft, many of the planes continued machine gunning the AA guns as they roared over the ship after the attack.

Geisler had asked for four direct hits from his aircrew. They gave him no less than six direct hits and three near-misses, a concentration of bombs that no ship, especially an aircraft-carrier, could be expected to live through. Capt Boyd described the attack as brilliantly executed and pressed home with the utmost skill and determination. By the time the last Stuka had thundered down and away through the flak-drenched sky, the *Illustrious* had staggered out of line, her steering gear crippled, her lifts smashed and her decks torn open and laid waste, her defensive armament wrecked.

At 1238hrs the first bomb smashed through the port number one pom-pom position, wrecking the guns and killing two of the crew. It sheared on through the ship's hull before exploding at water level, sending splinters up through the hull.

*Cunningham of Hyndhope; *A Sailors Odyssey*; Hutchinson, London.

Seconds later came the second hit, right
for'ard near to her bows, the bomb penetrating
the armoured flight-deck and bursting in the
paint store which ignited in a searing cloud
of flame. The stricken area was sealed off
and flooded by damage control parties and the
fire soon brought under control.

Another heavy bomb almost struck the
bridge island and smacked straight on to the
number one starboard pom-pom gun, killing
all its crew and tearing the gun from its
mounting. It also decimated the crew of S2
pom-pom and caused numerous casualties
among the ammunition supply parties with
flying fragments. The carrier itself could just
shrug off these hits, crippling although they
were to her defences.

The next bomb was a 1,100lb armour-
piercing type, and the *Illustrious* was not
built to withstand such a weapon. It hit
directly on the after lift at 1240hrs, pulping a
Fulmar fighter and its young pilot who was
going down on it. Worse, for the lift was half-
way down into the well when the bomb struck,
and the impact tilted the lift over like a toy
before it collapsed, into the hangar deck;
huge scythes of metal smashed across the
hangar, cutting down men and tearing
through 13 aircraft stowed there. The after
gun bays were knocked out, their crews
suffering heavy casualties. All the after guns
fell silent. Torpedoes stacked in the hangar
threatened to ignite and add to the carnage.

Another 1,100lb bomb followed the first
down the lift-well at 1242hrs. It struck the
canted-up lift, slid off it at an angle and
detonated among the smouldering aircraft,
wiping out the assembled fire-fighters in an

instant. Ammunition and aviation fuel exploded and the fires rekindled with a renewed fury.

Almost at the same instant another armour-piercing bomb landed close alongside the yawing ship, bursting level with the for'ard lift which burst upward in a drunken arc. The ship was still making considerable speed and the resulting draught swept through this archway fanning the blaze in the after hangar. Smoke and flame swept over the *Illustrious* but her ordeal was not yet over.

A second wave of Stukas bored in and with no flak left to stop them another 1,000-pounder burst on the after flight-deck, tearing through the armour-plated deck and exploding deep in the ship's vitals. The wardroom, filled with off-duty officers, was wiped out and the ammunition conveyor was written off. All the lights went out and new fires added to the inferno, fed by fuel from the broken pipes and blazing aircraft.

Her engines, however, almost miraculously had not been touched and she was still capable of 17kts. Coupled with the task of getting her fires under control was added the battle to get the ship itself under control. Eventually, after Herculean efforts, she was brought on a course, steering by engines only. Her only hope of salvation lay in getting her into Malta dockyard. Only here could sufficient repairs be done to enable her to get away to Alexandria. The question now was would the Luftwaffe allow it?

The two battleships had come off lightly, for with their stronger batteries of high-angled guns they had been able to beat off the diversionary attack. but even so the *Warspite*

was hit a glancing blow by a 550lb bomb which failed to detonate completely and she suffered only superficial damage.

Cunningham detached the destroyers *Hasty* and *Jaguar* from the screen to provide the carrier with a close escort and her airborne fighters flew off to Malta where they hastily refuelled and rearmed and returned to cover their crippled ship. The battle fleet remained in the close vicinity ready to provide an anti-aircraft screen and by 1600hrs, sure enough, the Stukas returned to finish the job.

Thirteen attacked at 1600hrs and 14 at 1710hrs but apart from scoring a near-miss on the *Valiant*, which caused some casualties, they failed to cause further damage to the *Illustrious* and by 2145hrs that evening she had arrived off Malta and was taken into the dockyard under tow.

There followed 13 days of intensive work by the dockyard to repair her sufficiently to get away to the safety of Alexandria. It was a desperate race against time, for Fliegerkorps X mounted attack after attack against the ship as she lay helpless alongside Parlatorio Wharf. Day after day the Ju87s hammered in, braving the heavy flak defences of Valletta harbour and the fighters from the neighbouring airfields.

The whole dockside area around her berth was pounded into rubble and on 16 January 44 Stukas attacked, scoring yet another direct hit with a 1,100lb bomb which exploded close to the after lift well, further adding to the devastation of their previous hits. On the 18th the dive-bombers switched their attack to the airfields at Hal Far and Luqa and 51 of them pounded them to rubble. Still the

Above: The ordeal of *Illustrious*. While the crippled carrier was undergoing rush repairs in Valetta Dockyard (right-centre) the Stukas tried to finish her off./*IWM*

work on the ship was pressed ahead, her steering gear was rigged up, her broken hull was pumped out and the splinter holes plugged and then, having silenced the fighter defences, 42 Ju87s came in on the 19th and planted two heavy bombs close alongside the *Illustrious* which hurled her hard against the wharf, holing her under water and fracturing her port turbine. The Germans lost five dive-bombers in these raids.

Day and night the work continued during a lull in the attacks, and on the evening of 23 January, 13 days after the first assault, the carrier crept out to sea and signalled down for full speed ahead. Steaming at 25kts she reached Alexandria two days later. It was a tremendous episode and a magnificent tribute to the men who had built her, for by all accounts she should have been sunk. As it was she was out of the war for almost a year undergoing a virtual rebuilding in America, and, to take her place, her newly completed sister ship, the *Formidable*, was sent to join Cunningham's fleet; but profiting by the *Illustrious*'s misfortune, she was sent via the Cape to avoid the Sicilian Channel, now acknowledged as Stuka territory. For while *Illustrious* battled to stay afloat, the victorious Gruppen had not been content with merely neutralising a carrier.

During their attacks on Valletta harbour the Stukas had not only caused serious damage to the dockyard but had inflicted further casualties on the Navy. On the 16th one of the merchant ships of the convoy, the *Essex*, had taken a bomb through her engine-room and the cruiser *Perth* was near-missed and damaged. Cunningham sailed the rest of the fleet for Alexandria. Meanwhile the fleet had suffered another grievous blow.

On 11 January, after escorting the damaged destroyer *Gallant* into the dubious safety of Valletta harbour, Rear-Adm Renouf's cruisers, *Gloucester* and *Southampton*, with the destroyers *Defender* and *Diamond*, were steering eastward to join the main fleet. None of the ships were fitted with radar and everyone was certain that they were now out of Stuka range.

They were not. They had been sighted earlier and now, led by a Heinkel He111, 12 Stukas of Maj Enneccerus's II/StG2 surprised the two cruisers in an attack from out of the sun in position 34° 54′ N, 18° 24′ E, almost 300 miles east of the Sicilian bases.

Splitting into two groups the dive-bombers plummetted down on the two ships and scored two hits on the *Southampton*. One bomb ploughed through her wardroom and the second smashed into the petty-officers' mess. By cruel chance both were crowded with off-duty officers and men relaxing in what they thought was a safe area. The loss of life aboard was very heavy. Large fires were started over the engine-rooms which rapidly got out of control and spread, and by 1605hrs she had come to a halt.

The *Gloucester* also took a large bomb in this raid, which pierced the roof of the director control tower and wrecked the bridge. Luckily it failed to explode but even so the damage was extensive and nine men were killed and 14 wounded. *Southampton* had finally to be abandoned and be sunk by our own forces. Her survivors were taken aboard the *Gloucester* and *Diamond*. She was the largest ship to be sunk by air attack up to that time. being of 10,000 tons and only completed three years earlier.

The crippling of the *Illustrious* and the sinking of the *Southampton* were early confirmation to the Germans of the effectiveness of the dive-bomber units against even the most modern warships and caused some consternation in the fleet. Back in England the talk was of the uselessness of the Stukas after the Battle of Britain, but the men of the Mediterranean Fleet no longer held such cosy illusions. Not for over two years did the Royal Navy sail any warship larger than a cruiser through the Sicilian Straits.

Lack of warship targets did not mean the end of operations by the Ju87s, for the subjection of Malta was high on their list of

Above: An Italian Stuka on the grass field of Apulia field in southern Italy in 1941. /*N. Malizia*

Above right: Mahlke's torn-up Stuka back on its Sicilian airfield after his adventures over Malta./*Archiv Schliephake*

Right: A Stuka of 4 Staffel II/StG77 with its 50kg bombs fitted with Dinortstab extended percussion fuses. /*Archiv Schliephake*

Below right: Another view of a 50kg Dinortstab equipped aircraft of II/StG77. Dinort was an Oberstleutnant, and his unit invented these extended fuses in Greece in 1941. /*Wolfinger via Archiv Schliephake*

Bottom right: Aircraft of 7/StG77 with the Dinortstab fused bombs. /*Archiv Schliephake*

priorities. Helmut Mahlke relates on a typical Stuka mission over Malta during the attacks launched against the British airfields on 26 February, 1941. During his dive a direct hit by flak punched an enormous area of his starboard inner wing out but left the dive flap intact. Somehow the sturdily built aircraft survived:

'I was hit during my dive attack, just after bomb release, at very low altitude. I recovered my aircraft from the dive using full controls, full power and manual trim. When we levelled out I found myself heading toward a large hangar on my target airfield. The doors of the hangar loomed invitingly open and inside I could see three aircraft undergoing maintenance. I thought, "These are my last moments", but they were not! My aircraft started to climb in the last seconds and I passed a few scant feet over the hangar roof in safety, my landing gear cutting a telephone wire en route.

'I headed south through a valley and came clear. After passing over the southern coastline of Malta I turned west out to sea but was not far from the shore when I was taken under fighter attack by a Hurricane. This fighter made five deliberate runs on my unmanoeuvrable aircraft, and later we found that he had scored 42 hits on it. Before he could complete his work he was shot down by a Bf109 of our fighter escort which had spotted my plight.

'I had taken off from Comiso at 1315hrs and finally got my aircraft safely down there again at 1445hrs, landing the machine with full power on since it was obvious that I stood no chance of getting her down and level with anything less. But the Ju87 made it and I could not agree more that, for its purpose, the Stuka was a sturdy and exceptionally strong aircraft.'

They were also needed to smash British tanks and guns and lead Rommel's first offensive in the desert, and in February Fliegerkorps Afrika was formed under the command of Gen Frohlich with 20 Bf110 twin-engined fighters and about 50 Stukas from StG2. Even although used mainly in the ground attack rôle they were able to show their strength over the sea when called upon, and among the warships sunk off North Africa in the period February to May were the monitor *Terror*, the destroyer *Dainty* and the minesweeper *Huntley*.

'The German dive-bombers', recalled Adm Cunningham, 'were a menace.'

They were to prove to be more than just that, for before too long they were able to dispute the control of the Mediterranean Sea, not just over Malta and the Sicilian Channel, but over the whole Eastern Basin.

6 The Killing Ground

When, on 6 April 1941, the German armies swept into the Balkans, Jugoslavia and Greece, it was with the usual breathtaking speed and efficiency they had displayed earlier, and, despite the numerous examples which lay before them, these two small nations were equally unable to withstand this high-speed type of warfare. Spearheading the rapid drive south, which swept all before it, were, as before, the ground-attack elements of Gen Freiherr von Richthofen's VII Air Corps. This force included three Stukagruppen, two flown in from France and one from Africa the preceding March. In all, some 150 dive-bombers had been concentrated on Bulgarian airfields in a matter of days.

The dive-bombers' contribution to the quick victories was paramount and among their successes were the sinking of the Greek battleship *Kilkis* and the destroyer *Psara* in dock at Salamis on 23 April which effectively crippled the small Greek Navy. By the 27th, Athens had fallen and the British Army was pulling out from the mainland.

The bulk of the Allied forces were re-established on the island of Crete which had already been occupied by British troops since the previous March. They now set to, in the time left to them, to increase the island's defences. In Berlin it was Crete's great strategical potential as an offensive base for long-range bombers which most perturbed Hitler, and he expressed great uneasiness that it would thus provide suitable bases for aircraft operating against the rich Rumanian oilfields.

With his planned final settlement with the Soviet Union imminent, he could not rest easy, and into his fears came the suggestion from Air-General Löhr, commanding Luft-flotte 4, and from Generalleutnant Student, commander of XI Air Corps, that such resistance as the British might offer could be overcome by taking the island from the air. Keitel and others stated that, should such a

Right: In the brief Balkan campaign, which crushed Yugoslavia and Greece, the Stukas again led the major breakthroughs./*Franz Selinger*

66

move be contemplated, then the obvious target was Malta, not Crete, but the idea found favour in the Führer's thoughts and after brief consultation with Mussolini, he set the wheels turning with his Directive No 28.

Einsatz Merkur involved the use of no less than 530 Ju52 transports and meant the movement of Fliegerkorps XI, which was based in central Germany, down to Athens, a move which was completed in the startling time of three weeks. The date of the attack was set for 20 May and in the meantime additional airfields were levelled around Athens to accommodate the huge number of parachute-dropping Junkers transports and gliders required.

To pave the way for these, Fliegerkorps VIII could deploy over 600 aircraft of all types, and the dive-bomber units were concentrated in the forward areas at new bases, Mulaoi, Melos, Scarpanto and Corinth and Argos. Attacks started at 0700hrs on the morning of 20 May when the Stukas, supported by medium bombers and twin-engined fighters, made very heavy attacks on the British defence works around Maleme and Canea with a view to disposing of the anti-aircraft defences.

An hour later the initial airborne troops went in supported by further waves of Stukas and fighters in the ground attack rôle. Resistance was fiercer than had been expected and objectives which should have been taken on Day One were not secured. To the British defenders it appeared 'inconceivable' that airborne troops alone could invade an island

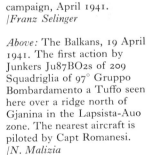

Top: A Ju87B over the River Strummer in the Balkan campaign, April 1941. /*Franz Selinger*

Above: The Balkans, 19 April 1941. The first action by Junkers Ju87BO2s of 209 Squadriglia of 97° Gruppo Bombardamento a Tuffo seen here over a ridge north of Gjanina in the Lapsista-Auo zone. The nearest aircraft is piloted by Capt Romanesi. /*N. Malizia*

Left: A pair of Junkers Ju87B-2s of 208 Squadriglia, 101° Gruppo Autonomo B. a T. over the mountains of Albania during the Greek campaign in 1940./*N. Malizia*

150 miles long by 20 miles wide and occupy it against a pre-warned defence. Sea support must be forthcoming, they reasoned, and the Mediterranean Fleet immediately moved in to take up intercepting positions around the island to prevent this happening.

Unfortunately the British appreciation was wrong, very few ship-borne troops were involved, the whole action was planned and carried out by Luftwaffe units and the German Army was not consulted. A few small convoys did sail but these were not essential to the main operation.

The stage was thus set for what was to be the bloodiest confrontation yet between the Royal Navy and Richthofen's Stukas.

The naval side of the campaign opened encouragingly for Adm Cunningham's fleet. During the 20th, reconnaissance reports had indicated several small convoys southbound from the Aegean area towards Crete, and light forces were accordingly despatched that evening to maintain patrols north of the island during the night with a view to intercepting these.

First blood went to Force C, comprising the light cruisers *Naiad* and *Perth* and destroyers *Kandahar, Kingston, Juno* and *Nubian,* which, under the command of Vice-Adm E. L. S. King, was ordered to pass through the Kaso Strait and make a search through the sea off Stampalia then to concentrate off Heraklion at dawn on the 21st. While traversing the Kaso Strait, it encountered an Italian force of MAS-boats* which it engaged and drove off. By 0600hrs Adm King was retiring through the Kaso Straits after being joined by the cruiser *Calcutta.*

Meanwhile Force E, consisting of the destroyers *Jervis, Nizam* and *Ilex,* had bombarded Scarpanto airfield during the

*E-Boat types.

night and was also steering to join Adm King. The Luftwaffe, although aware of the presence of the British Mediterranean Fleet, was too busy supporting its hard-pressed paratroops ashore to divert any large part of its force to attack the ships. During the morning of the 21st, Force C was shadowed and one Stuka Gruppe despatched to strike it.

This unit, StG2 under the command of Hauptmann Brücker, was based on the island of Scarpanto and had not enjoyed the visitation paid them by the British destroyers that night. Adm King's force had been bombed continuously from 0950hrs by medium bombers, German and Italian, but it was not until Brücker's vengeful Stukas arrived on the scene that the ships suffered any damage.

The Ju87s found Force C at 1245hrs, well to the south-east of Crete. King's orders were to patrol close to the island at night but to withdraw at daybreak. On this occasion his vessels were still within Stuka range and paid the price.

The dive-bombers concentrated on the destroyer *Juno* (1,690 ton), and despite desperate evasive action she was struck at 1249hrs by three bombs. The first two struck her aft and demolished her boiler-room and engine-rooms and opened them up to the sea, while the third penetrated her after magazine. The resulting explosion tore her apart and she went down in less than two minutes.

Loss of life was heavy, but fortunately the *Kandahar*, *Kingston* and *Nubian* were able to rescue six officers and 91 ratings from her complement, including her commanding officer, Cdr St. J. R. J. Tyrwhitt. Still under attack, the light forces withdrew still farther to the south and regrouped with the main battle fleet south-west of Kithera. There the fleet remained throughout the day while the fighting ashore continued unabated.

The Germans, regardless of losses, were flying in a constant stream of reinforcements and StG2 was in constant demand to carry out close support missions ashore to blast away the defences holding up the paratroops from their principal objectives, the main airfields.

Further sightings were received by Adm Cunningham's commander afloat, Adm Rawlings, and that evening the light forces were again formed into three striking forces and sent north of Crete to engage. Both Force C and D, the latter of which consisted of the cruisers *Dido*, *Orion* and *Ajax* (which had been damaged by bombing during the day), and destroyers *Hereward*, *Janus*, *Hasty* and *Kimberley* under the command of Rear-Adm Glennie, were sent to find a reported convoy, while Force B, *Gloucester* and *Fiji*, with the destroyers *Greyhound* and *Griffin*, commanded by Capt Rowley, was sent through the Kithera Strait to the north-west of Crete.

It was Force D which finally located the invasion force. This comprised an Italian-German squadron with the resounding title of the First Caique Squadron, and consisted of 20 of these little vessels under the command of Lt Oesterlin of the German Navy. They were carrying 4,000 troops from Milos which were destined to land to the west of Maleme that night. They had a naval escort of two Italian torpedo-boats.

At 2330hrs on the 21st, while some 18 miles north of Canae, this motley collection was sighted by the destroyer *Janus*. One of the Italian escorts fired two torpedoes, which were avoided, and the *Dido* and *Ajax* then blew her out of the water. The way then lay open for a vigorous two-hour free-for-all with the British squadron getting in among the German vessels with gun, pom-pom and ram. Under the glare of the warships' searchlights it

Below: The Greek campaign of 1941 was another brief demonstration of the efficiency of the Luftwaffe. A Stuka attack on shipping at Piraeus. /*Ullstein*

Right: In the Tirana region of Albania during the Balkans Campaign on 14 March 1941. Italian Stuka piloted by Lt Carlo Seganti en route to the target area./*N. Malizia*

Below: A pair of Junkers Ju87B2s of 208 Squadriglia. /*N. Malizia*

Bottom: A large formation of Stukas from 101° Gruppo return to their base after an attack on Greek artillery positions./*AMI via N. Malizia*

appeared that great destruction had been done and it was thought at the time that the entire German unit of 4,000 men had been annihilated.

Despite the fact that two steamers, a dozen caiques and other diverse craft were either sunk or left ablaze, some 10 caiques survived by fleeing and hiding among the islands. Only 300 soldiers actually lost their lives, but this put an end to this attempt at seaborne reinforcement for the time being. Once again the Royal Navy had shown that it commanded the sea. Until the Stukas could prove otherwise, the movement of Axis shipping over the waters around Crete was suicidal.

Although his mission had proven highly successful, Rear-Adm Glennie was now faced with a difficult decision. Careful check among the cruisers of his command revealed that the *Dido*, his principal AA ship, had expended 70% of her anti-aircraft ammunition, while *Orion* and *Ajax* had used 62 and 58% of theirs, respectively. It was plain that if he lingered any longer in the Aegean he would run the risk of exposing his squadron to heavy air attack with which he would be unable to cope. Adm Sir Andrew Cunningham was informed of the situation and ordered Glennie to pull his ships out and return to base at Alexandria to replenish.

Meanwhile Capt Rowley, with his two cruisers and two destroyers, was falling back on the main fleet which was patrolling some 45 miles south-west of the Kithera Channel. This consisted of the battleships *Warspite* (flag) and *Valiant*, a cruiser and several destroyers. However, Adm King's squadron had not withdrawn and following his previous

orders, which were not countermanded when Glennie withdrew, he was still searching northward of Crete.

At 0830hrs the ships of this force sighted a single caique, which had become detatched from another German convoy, south of Milo. The *Perth* quickly sank her but heavy and prolonged air attacks developed by Ju88s and Do17s. Despite this King pressed on towards the main bulk of the enemy convoy and at 1010 hrs he sighted it. The cruisers drove off one of the escorting torpedo-boats while the destroyer *Kingston* engaged the second, scoring two hits.

The convoy was now wide open but the air attacks were unceasing and King knew his AA ammunition was dwindling alarmingly. He therefore withdrew, but not before the convoy had been dispersed and also put back, although it was unharmed.

Adm Rawlings, on learning of Force C's difficulties, steered to meet it and to provide fire support and at 1321hrs contact was made. King had meanwhile taken bomb damage on the *Naiad* and the *Carlisle*, the latter losing her captain. These attacks were supplemented by fighter-bomber assaults by Bf109s, one of which planted a bomb in the *Warspite* at 1332hrs and completely wrecked her starboard secondary and anti-aircraft batteries.

Force B was also falling back under attack to join the main fleet. It was bombed heavily and both cruisers were slightly damaged, but they joined Rawling's flag at 0830hrs. Other reinforcements were also on their way; from Malta came the 5th Destroyer Flotilla, *Kelly, Kashmir, Kipling, Kelvin* and *Jackal*, under Capt Mountbatten; they joined at 1600hrs.

The 14th Flotilla, *Jervis, Nizam* and *Ilex*, and the 10th Flotilla, *Stuart, Voyager* and *Vendetta* were also despatched post-haste from Alexandria to assist.

But the Stukas were gathering also. Under the command of Oberstleutnant Dinort at Molai there were two Gruppen of StG2 available for action against the fleet. Both these were despatched from their bases at Mycene and Molai at 0530hrs led by Oberstleutnants Hitschold and Seigeland. It had been these Stukas which had attacked the cruisers of Capt Rowley earlier without scoring; but now they had returned to their bases, bombed-up, refuelled and by midday they were ready, in conjunction with Brücker's unit from Scarpanto, to concentrate their assaults on the imposing fleet now gathered to the south of Kithera.

Joining them in the attacks were Ju88s, Do17s, He111s, Bf109s and Bf110s of all the units engaged in subjecting Crete. Richthofen decreed an all-out effort while the good clear weather conditions lasted.

At 1320hrs a solitary caique was sighted between Pori and Antikithera islands and the destroyer *Greyhound* was detached to destroy it. This she did, but the price extracted for this one small boat was to prove exorbitant, for eight Ju87s pounced on the *Greyhound* while she was returning alone and unsupported. Twisting and turning violently she evaded several attacks but it was all in vain. At 1351hrs, in sight of the main fleet, one Stuka planted a 550lb bomb on a 3in AA gun amidships and two 100lb fragmentation bombs also scored hits. The destroyer sank in four minutes, all her boats and rafts having been destroyed save for her whaler which she managed to launch.

Adm King sent the *Kandahar* and *Kingston* to rescue the survivors and then, not realising that *Gloucester* and *Fiji* had only 18 and 30% of their anti-aircraft ammunition respectively, left to them, sent these two cruisers to act as support. When finally informed of the state of the anti-aircraft supplies aboard the two ships Adm Rawlings at once told them to rejoin as soon as possible, but it was then too late. That solitary caique was to cost the Fleet dear. Aided by waves of Ju88s, StG2 now proceeded to concentrate on this little group, which was soon reduced to firing practise shells at their tormentors. Near-misses further damaged the *Gloucester* (9,900 ton), but at 1550, some nine miles off Pori, in sight of the fleet, a Stuka hit her several times and she came to a standstill her decks demolished and heavily on fire.

With *Fiji* out of AA ammunition and the two destroyers low on oil fuel there was no alternative but to leave her, but this did not save her companion. Both forces were now pulling out quickly to escape this pounding and at 1645hrs the *Valiant* was hit. Badly damaged and brought to a standstill by a bomb from a Bf109 piloted by an officer from the crack I/LG2 Gruppe, the *Fiji* (8,000 ton)

was finally finished off at 1915hrs by another bomb which brought down her mast and tore open her decks from end to end.

The two destroyers could not tarry but threw over their Carley rafts and sped off to join the fleet. They did, however, return after dark and carried out a prolonged search for the *Fiji*'s survivors. *Kandahar* rescued 184 and *Kingston* 339. Many others were picked up by the German air-sea rescue planes and Italian torpedo-boats the next day.

Nor was this the end of the total kills for StG2. Although the losses had all been caused by detaching small units from the main fleet, this lesson was still not appreciated. That evening the 5th Flotilla was sent out on its own (*Kelvin* and *Jackal* had been previously detached) to patrol into Canae Bay. En route the *Kipling* developed a steering defect and *Kelly* and *Kashmir* pressed on alone.

The 14th Flotilla was likewise despatched to patrol off Heraklion while the *Decoy* and *Hero* were sent to embark the King of Greece from Agriarumeli. These latter movements pointed the way to how things were going ashore. Nevertheless, reinforcements continued to be taken into Crete.

Only two ships of the 5th Flotilla made contact with the enemy; they sank a single caique and then proceeded to carry out a brief bombardment of Maleme airfield, now

Below left: A sequence shot by Luftwaffe men as the dying cruiser *Gloucester* set ablaze by repeated dive-bomber hits, keels over and sinks./*IWM*

Below: Crete, May 1941. The 10,000 ton cruiser *Gloucester* is pinned down by Stuka bombs off the disputed island./*IWM*

in German hands. While withdrawing they came across and fired upon a second caique, leaving it on fire.

At 0408hrs, after examining detailed reports received on the loss of the *Gloucester* and *Fiji*, and on the state of the remainder of the fleet's anti-aircraft capability, Adm Cunningham ordered all forces to withdraw to Alexandria. In fact he had been misled, for the battleships still had adequate supplies of ammunition, but this withdrawal left the various destroyer forces unsupported during the morning of the 23rd, a fact which was soon noted and seized upon by the Luftwaffe.

Dornier bombers of KG2 located the *Kelly* and *Kashmir* at first light and delivered two attacks which the destroyers evaded without much difficulty. But nemesis was approaching in the form of 24 Stukas commanded by Hauptmann Hitschold. They located Mountbatten's ships at 0755hrs and immediately dived to attack.

Almost as once the *Kashmir* (1,690 ton) was hit by a heavy bomb, heeled over and sank in two minutes. She managed to shoot down one of her assailants. Next the *Kelly*, turning under full helm, was struck by a 1,100lb bomb. She was steaming in excess of 30kts and the momentum threw her right over to port, whereupon she capsized while still moving at speed. Her hull floated for

Top: Long-range Junkers Ju87Rs in the Balkans with their distinctive yellow noses and tail fins./*Archiv Schliephake*

Above: A yellow-nosed Ju87B over a Balkan port target in 1941. /*Archiv Schliephake*

Left: Ju87 'Richards' in the Balkans./*Archiv Schliephake*

Above: A clear ground view of the Stuka, port side, in standard Luftwaffe markings. /IWM

20 minutes upside down before she finally sank.

Fortunately for the survivors the *Kipling* was in the vicinity, having completed her repairs, and witnessed the attack. She stormed up in the midst of the attack and managed to avoid being hit. It was now a case of careful ship handling as during the next three hours this destroyer was subjected to a further six attacks by high-level bombers. Despite this she rescued no less than 128 men from the *Kelly* and 153 from *Kashmir*, including both ships' captains.

She finally left for Alexandria at 1100hrs heavily laden, and was subjected to no less than 40 more bombing attacks, during which she estimated 83 bombs were aimed at her. The plucky little vessel finally ran out of fuel some 50 miles from base, but the netlayer *Protector* came out and towed her to safety. It was a gallant episode.

It could not make up for the loss of another two destroyers, however nor for the fact that reinforcements for the islands' garrison could not be landed by daylight. The losses to the fleet had been prohibitive and it now remained to see whether or not the Germans could pull off the seemingly impossible and take the island by air-power alone. All too quickly it

became apparent that they could – and with ease.

Fighting continued to be fierce ashore throughout the 25th and 26th and all the time the endless conveyer belt of Ju52s rolled up the captured runways and disgorged fresh waves of troops. In order to relieve the hard-pressed defenders, the Navy decided to launch an aerial attack on the Stuka base at Scarpanto. The aircraft-carrier *Formidable* had been at Alexandria during the initial operations, unable to participate because her Fulmar fighter aircraft had been reduced to a total of four operational machines during previous convoy runs to Malta. Now, by scraping together every flyable plane, most of them of dubious ability, she could muster 12, which would give her and the fleet a token defence. It was planned to use four Swordfish as bombers and follow them up with four Fulmars in the ground-strafing rôle. It was a mere pin-prick but the RAF was quite unable to offer even this and the C-in-C felt that, if surprise was achieved, they could get away with it.

Formidable therefore sailed from Alexandria at noon on the 25th, escorted by the battleships *Queen Elizabeth* and *Barham* and the destroyers *Jervis*, *Janus*, *Kandahar*, *Nubian*,

Hasty, *Voyager* and *Vendetta* (the *Decoy* joined later). The force was fortunately undetected during its approach and between 0500hrs and 0600hrs from a position 100 miles south of the island of Scarpanto, the carrier launched her puny strike force.

The eight Fleet Air Arm aircraft arrived over the German base undetected and succeeded in destroying two bombers, while damaging, in varying degrees, five others, mainly Italian Cr42 biplanes. Although these losses were not to cause Hauptmann Brücker much hardship, it was nevertheless a nasty surprise to the Germans, for they had no idea that the carrier was operational.

It was not expected that the Luftwaffe would take this affront lightly and indeed the fleet was subjected to much reconnaissance throughout the forenoon, but the ships rapidly withdrew out of range of the Greek-based Stukas.

It had been overlooked, however, that Ju87s were still operating in Libya. It was bad luck for the British on this day for 20 Ju87s of II/StG2, under Maj Enneccerus, happened to be on patrol in search of shipping in the southern approaches to Crete. The Gruppe was at the extreme length of its range when it sighted the fleet at 1320hrs. At once the carrier turned into the wind to fly off her remaining serviceable Fulmars – there were only two left – but she had no time, and before they could get into an intercepting position Maj Enneccerus led his Stukas into the attack.

Not only had the Mediterranean Fleet come up against the Stukas unexpectedly but their opponents also proved to be their skilful enemies of January and II/StG2 was delighted with the opportunity to mete out to *Formidable* the same treatment that they had given her sister ship on that occasion.

Enneccerus himself scored a direct hit with the first bomb of the attack which hit the carrier forward on her flight-deck. Eight Stukas followed their leader down against the carrier and she was hit again on the starboard side, aft. The bulkheads between numbers 17 and 24 bulkheads were blown out, X 4·5in gun turret was demolished with heavy casualties and the ship's launching accelerator damaged. Nevertheless the carrier succeeded in bringing the resulting fires under control and was able to recover her aircraft, but once again the Mediterranean Fleet's only aircraft-carrier was severely hit after only one sortie and again the fleet was deprived of even her meagre fighter cover.

The other dive-bombers had concentrated on the two battleships and other escorts, but the capital ships escaped damage. Not so fortunate was the screening destroyer *Nubian* (1,890 ton). She was struck fair and square aft right on her depth-charge stowage which immediately erupted in a sheet of flame 200ft high and wiped out X and Y gun mounts as well as blowing her whole stern section away. Remarkably, her engines continued to function and, steering by her propellers and guarded by her flotilla leader, *Jervis*, she eventually managed to limp back to harbour after everything disposable had been dumped overboard to lighten the ship.

Maj Enneccerus's force suffered no losses in this textbook attack and all II/StG2 aircraft returned to their desert base. Again, in one brief encounter, the Stukas had shown their power against even the main units of the fleet. Adm Cunningham was in a cruel dilemma. Not to have put to sea would have meant abandoning the troops ashore to their fate, but to go on operating without air cover against the Stukas would mean the eventual crippling of his entire fleet, upon which hung the fate of Malta and ultimately the Middle East.

When the fleet returned to Alexandria on the 27th it had already suffered further casualties when the *Barham* had been hit on Y turret by a bomb from LG1's Ju88s. It was on this day that General Wavell, despite considerable exhortation to the contrary by the Prime Minister earlier, came to the conclusion that the battle ashore was lost. He signalled the War Cabinet to this effect and it was decided to evacuate the island. Far from easing the Mediterranean Fleet's burden, this decision was to increase it. Now it was fully committed to picking up the troops from the exposed southern beaches of Crete with the sky dominated by the German Air Force. This was no Dunkirk, true, the numbers of troops to be lifted were far fewer, but the distance they had to be hauled under constant air attack was much greater.

It was clear that even more casualties could be expected, even though the actual embarkation would be restricted to night-time only. Nevertheless the Navy squared its shoulders and got on with the task.

The first lifts started well; two forces, one for Heraklion and one for Sphakia, left Alexandria on the 28th, loaded, and resailed unharmed the next morning before dawn. Four destroyers, *Napier*, *Nizam*, *Kelvin* and *Kandahar*, embarked almost 3,000 men and brought them back to Egypt without loss, but the force for Heraklion suffered a disaster.

Under the command of Adm Rawlings, Force B, as the squadron was code-named, consisted of the cruisers *Orion*, *Ajax* and *Dido* and the destroyers *Jackal*, *Kimberley*, *Hereward*, *Hotspur*, *Imperial* and *Decoy*. It was still some 90 miles from Scarpanto when the Luftwaffe found it in daylight and before dusk fell it had been subjected to all manner of air

Above: Sharp clean profile of the Ju87 on the deck. Note markings./*IWM*

Right: Among Germany's allies the Stuka was widely used. This machine is of the Hungarian 102/1 Zuhanobömbezo Szezad formed in 1943 with Berthas./*Archive Govi*

Below right: A Ju87D of the Rumanian Air Force at Briansk airfield. /*Bundesarchiv*

attack. At 1920hrs the *Imperial* had been near-missed and at 2100hrs the *Ajax* was damaged for the second time and sent back to Gibraltar.

Nightfall brought some rest for the hard-pressed squadron and between 2330hrs and 0300hrs on the 29th, it was occupied in embarking the whole of the Heraklion garrison some 4,000 soldiers. It sailed 20 minutes later, for it was clear that it must be as far away from the Stuka airfields as possible before daybreak, but soon after it had got under way the *Imperial*'s steering gear broke down and she almost collided with the two cruisers. The destroyer proved incapable of steering and Adm Rawlings concluded that she must be sacrificed to enable the rest of the ships to clear the area by dawn. The *Hotspur* accordingly took off the 400 troops and her crew and sank her. But even this brief enforced halt was to prove fatal.

The ships were still steering south through the Kaso Strait when the first Ju87s arrived overhead and began their dives on the destroyer screen at first light. Four aircraft picked the *Hereward* as their target, but she successfully avoided the bombs of the first three. The fourth made no mistake, diving to under 1,500ft in a determined attack. A 550lb bomb struck the *Hereward* abaft her fore funnel, which was almost knocked overboard, and she swung out of line. Rawlings had little choice but to leave her and she was last seen making for Crete where her captain hoped to beach her. She eventually sank but the majority of her crew got ashore and were taken prisoner. In the same attack a Stuka bomb near-missed another destroyer, the *Decoy*, reducing her speed to 25kts, and, at 0700hrs, the *Orion* also had a narrow escape.

Fighter cover arranged for daybreak over the Kaso Strait failed to materialise, and soon further formations of StG2 appeared overhead. The Gruppe was now flying continuous shuttle services between the fleet and their bases, pausing only to bomb-up and refuel. The attacks were intense and vicious and accurate anti-aircraft fire failed to prevent further casualties among Rawling's force.

At 0735hrs a Stuka pulled out of its dive and passing close over the *Orion* sprayed the cruiser's bridge with machine gun fire, killing Capt G. R. B. Back. At 0815hrs another Ju87 scored a direct hit on the *Dido*, wrecking B turret, and less than an hour later the *Orion* took a 550lb bomb on A turret. In both cases the gun turrets were demolished and heavy casualties inflicted on the unfortunate troops herded aboard the ships.

The final attacks by the Scarpanto Stukas were made at the edge of the effective range, when the squadron was about 100 miles south-east of Kaso. Eleven dive-bombers concentrated on the smoking *Orion*, pressing in very close to land a devastating hit on the cruiser's bridge. The bomb plunged right through the bridge structure, putting the lower conning position out of action, and exploded in the stokers' messdeck. The *Orion* had more than 1,000 soldiers aboard and many of these were crammed into this space. The resulting carnage was appalling with the bloody carcasses of men pulped amongst the shattered and twisted steel of the former living space.

A strong fire broke out which was only controlled with difficulty and the ship sped along quite out of control, with her compasses, engine-room telegraphs, steering gear and three of her boilers wrecked. She took on a heavy list. The total casualties were impossible to estimate accurately, but it is thought that 260 men were killed and 280 wounded by that one bomb. All these attacks cost the Germans only one Ju87, to ships' gunfire.

Fortunately the ships were now out of range of the dive-bombers, and although medium bombers took up the attack they scored no hits and eventually two Fleet Air Arm Fulmars arrived to provide some sort of air cover. The badly battered Force B finally limped into Alexandria at 2000hrs, when *Orion* had 10 tons of fuel and two 6in shells left.

This was the final operation in which the Ju87 took part. Further embarkations of troops took place on the nights of 29/30 May and 31 May/1 June, during which Ju88s hit the *Perth* and sank the anti-aircraft cruiser *Calcutta*, but the Stukas were being prepared for their next big operation, Barbarossa.

There can be no doubt that Operation Mercury was a signal victory for StG2 and that the Mediterranean Fleet paid an inflated price for its lack of fighter cover. Richthofen recorded: 'The result was abundantly clear. I was convinced that we had scored a great and decisive victory.'

With which Adm Cunningham was forced to agree: 'That the fleet suffered disastrously in this encounter with the unhampered German Air Force is evident, but it has to be remembered that on the credit side the Navy's duty was achieved and no enemy ship, whether warship or transport, succeeded in reaching Crete or intervening the battle in those critical days.'*

A final gleam of satisfaction for the defeated British was that in taking Crete the German parachute and glider forces suffered heavy losses themselves and never again was such an ambitious project mounted by Gen Student's crack units.

*Cunningham of Hyndhope; *A Sailors Odyssey*; Hutchinson, London.

7 Training, Techniques and Tactics

In view of the phenomenal successes the dive-bomber achieved, both as a ground-attack weapon and as a ship-buster in the early years of the war, it is of interest to take a brief look at what went into making a Stuka crew and what tactics the Ju87 bomber pilots developed over this period.

Prewar training in the Luftwaffe was quite vigorous and is regarded to have been, at the outbreak of the war, of a higher standard than any other air-arm. Centralised control and the formation of a special training inspectorate at the German Air Ministry laid the foundations for this and under the dynamic and totally dedicated flying instructors, Goering was able to initiate a large-scale recruitment of the cream of German youth for his fledgling Luftwaffe.

As may be expected from a country with Germany's military background, initial training was more in line with the Army than with the Air Force and was geared to create absolute disciplined men before turning them into aviators. Every recruit, including officer candidates, spent the first year of his training with a Flieger Ausbildungs Regiment where he would concentrate on military training and physical exercise. Only on lecture courses would he be taught the elementary principles of wireless and map-reading.

Infantry training would be accompanied by strict rules of no smoking and no drinking and the virtual restriction of all leisure periods to physical recreation and toughening exercises. With the welcome completion of this term the recruit would be drafted to a Fluganwaerter-kompanie, or recruit pool, where he would spend up to two months awaiting his flying training posting. This period would be filled by studying general aeronautical subjects before being transferred to an Elementary Flying Training School.

Here the pupil would get between 100 to 150 hours' flying in the biplane training types, of which about five hours were dual and 25 consisted of circuits and bumps, take-offs,

Below: A prewar training flight by a Ju87A-equipped Stukagruppen./*Ullstein*

Top right: A trainee Stuka pilot in front of his Ju87 Anton at Graz Stuka school in 1943. /*Wolfinger via Archiv Schliephake*

Centre right: The Anton was used for advance dive-bomber training during the war. Here a student pilot sits at the controls of his mount. /*Wolfinger via Archiv Schliephake*

Below right: An aircraft of the Stuka School, Tours, France. /*Archiv Schliephake*

simple banking turns and attempts at three-point landings. In conjunction with the flying lessons the technical and military programme was continued. It was during this period that recruits were watched closely by instructors who had to decide whether they were more suitable for fighters, bombers or dive-bombers, although in practise this was usually waived by the needs of the period.

A third term followed in which more emphasis was placed on the actual flying training, and all related subjects were studied; pupils were also seconded to operational units for short periods to gain first-hand knowledge of operational problems. Blind flying day and night in all weathers made sure that the Luftwaffe was less restricted by conditions of this nature than its fellows on the Continent. On completion of a stiff examination successful candidates were awarded their pilots certificates and their eagle badge, their 'wings'.

Those who were selected for dive-bombers underwent specialised training courses at dive-bomber schools, lasting for about four months. The officer cadets under instruction would make about 15 flights with an instructor before dive-bombing simulation solo. One such school was set up at Thalerhof near Graz in Austria soon after the Anschluss and was one of the first to be re-equipped with the Ju87, which replaced the ageing Henschel biplanes.

Dives were practised at angles of up to 90 degrees and the usual practise was for training dives to be made from 12,000ft with bomb-release and pull-out at 3,000ft, although this was ignored under war conditions when Stukas

usually went down much lower to ensure dead accuracy. Even so such tactics were tiring and the strain on trainees was great, so the maximum number of solo dives per day was restricted to 15.

Accuracy was the keynote of this course, but the cadets also underwent training in formation flying, aerial gunnery and other tactics of a more general nature. On completion of this course the cadet was commissioned as pilot-officer, and assigned to an operational unit. Due to the special emphasis placed on the dive-bomber in the prewar period by many senior Luftwaffe officers, including Goering himself, the Stuka units tended to attract a higher standard of cadet than the other bomber units, and this, coupled with the specialised training, tended to make them regard themselves as an élite, which feeling the first year of war certainly enhanced. On wartime Stuka training, Hans Drescher was trained at the Stuka School of Thalerhof, near Graz, Austria, in 1943, by which time the pressures of war in the East and the lack of fuel reserves were beginning to take effect. He recalls his training period in some detail: 'After finishing my basic flying training early in 1943 our group were asked to indicate individually which kind of squadron we would prefer to join.

'So we came to the Stuka Training School in Graz where we formed a group consisting of some 25 to 30 officers and non-commissioned officers. This group again divided into a smaller class of 10 pilots under one instructor, or as the War Academy listed them, supervisors. Here we underwent detailed training on a course lasting three months on the specialised use of the Ju87 ie diving, tactical formation and tactics, bomb dropping and shooting.

'To each group was attached a teaching officer and a flying officer. The School at that time had groups of three to five officers who taught and these were all highly decorated officers, most of them with *Ritterkreuz* and vast war and combat experience. For example Col Rudel was for a short time Commander of the Stuka School at Graz.

'At this stage of the war there were still many more volunteers for the Stuka units than could be accommodated, and only limited numbers of applicants were being accepted. The course was intensive and one constantly practised all the Stuka evolutions of diving and bomb accuracy until one reached the prescribed minimum standard. Naturally, depending on the ability of the trainees, the course varied in length slightly, but three months was considered the minimum required. In the case of those who failed to reach the standard required after that time they would normally be relegated to transportation squadrons. However, in special cases, the course would be prolonged.

'On completion of my three months course I piloted the Ju87-D as a qualified Stuka pilot and was instantly sent to Russia to a combat unit, the "Immelmann" unit, under the famous Rudel, and when with them I flew 130 dive-bomber sorties. I was wounded in action three times and decorated with the EK2 and the EK1, also the Deutsche Kreuz in Gold and the golden Frontflugspange award.

'Almost all of my training was done on the Ju87B at the school, and the normal form of attack was the same at the school as at the front, a steep dive from a height of 2,000m.

'The incident that most sticks in my memory from this training period was one of my first solo flights. I carried out my dive much too steeply and after pulling out I blacked out for quite a long time, or so it seemed. Even today I don't know how I could have survived it because I saw the trees within reach until I managed to climb to safety. I remember that I pulled and pulled and pulled on the joy-stick and I finally got to a safe altitude. I don't know exactly how low I went even now, but I was almost at ground level, and certainly not any higher than 100m.'

Helmut Mahlke lists the changes in these training schools which took place in the final years of the war.

'On 8 December, 1942 Stukaschule 1 was reorganised into StG101, which was named SG101 (Schlachtgeschwader 101) from 18 October 1943. This wing had three groups deployed on various bases, for example, Metz, Biblis, Orly, Clermont-Ferrand and, in September 1944, at Fassberg for re-equipping with the Fw190. By the end of 1944 the I/SG101 (which instructed initial pilot training

Below: A Stuka Staffel over the snow covered fields of East Prussia on a training flight. /*Ullstein*

Above left: Ju87Ds in formation over mountainous terrain./*Franz Selinger*

Left: Stark against the dawn sky a Stuka Staffel forms up. /*Bundesarchiv*

Below: A Ju87 heading east with a glider in tow. /*Archiv Schliephake*

on Ar96s) was at Wirschau, II/SGlol (Fw190s) at Brünn and III/SGlol (Fw190s) at Hörsching near Linz. The whole wing (SGlol) was disbanded on 27 December 1944.

'On 17 May 1943 the IV/Supplementary groups of the wings mentioned above were re-organised into Stuka Wing 151 at Agram. IV/StG1 from then on being I/StG151, IV/StG2 "Immelmann" became II/StG151, IV/StG3 became III/StG151, IV/StG77 became IV/StG151 and IV/StG5 became V/StG151. Each group contained two squadrons, then, on 27 December 1943, this wing was again reorgainsed into wing-staff with subordinate groups (I-III).

'There was also an SG152 which was brought together and incorporated into SG151, which from then on (7 August 1944) had four groups. Temporarily also there was an SG102 with a Stab and three squadrons and an SG103 at Metz, I and II/SG103 (at Fassberg, Diedenhofen, Biblis near Worms,

and then later just Fassberg and Hörsching).

'From December 1943 the Schlacht-fliegregeschwader 111 (SG111) took over from the Blindlugschule 11 (Instrument training centre) in the task of pilots instrument training. In this wing all the Nacht-schlachtflieger got their "do-it-yourself" method in the first units formed in the Eastern theatre.'

The Ju87 was an easy aircraft to fly but its low speed soon proved it to be an extremely vulnerable aircraft to the eight-gun fighters of the RAF. However, suitably protected and used in mass, the Stuka remained a formidable weapon right through the war. A hypothetical mission for a Ju87 crew on an antishipping strike would proceed as follows:

Following a briefing on the type of target, resistance expected and tactics to be used, the crew would board their aircraft where they normally, but not always, sat back-to-back.

The bomb-load would depend on the type of shipping to be brought under attack. One 550lb and four 60lb bombs were normal for attacking thin-skinned merchant vessels. 1,100lb armour piercing was customary against warship targets of cruiser size and upward which would be armoured to some extent, and later a special 2,000lb bomb was produced and adapted for Stuka use against battleships.

Take-off checking would be:

Tail trim at zero
Rudder trim indicator 90 from full right
Flaps to Start
Both main tanks on
Airscrew fully fine
Radiator and oil cooler open

Raids were mounted in various formations, Kette – three aircraft, Staffel – nine, Gruppe – 30 and Geschwader – 93 aircraft at full strength.

It is interesting to note that when a Stuka attack was mounted on warships up to the size of a light cruiser, a Staffel was used, but for a heavy cruiser or larger the whole Gruppen was employed.

A Kette, the smallest formation, consisted of a leader and two wingmen in position slightly astern; Kettenhunde* position this was called. For an attack in Staffel strength the Stukas would adopt a loose formation based on this with one Kette corresponding to the leader and two others taking formation as Kettenhunde.

Convoys were approached from a height of 13,000ft and at a speed of 150mph and bombing would take place at a height of 1,600ft with the Ju87 pulling out of its dive at around 700ft. With warships the tactics varied. Clover-leaf formations and continuous varying of flight levels were followed by attacks from several different directions against heavy ships with powerful anti-aircraft armaments. Destroyers on the other hand, capable of high speeds and manoeuvrability, were approached from astern where the Stuka

*Chained Dog.

Right: A pair of Ju87Bs in a practice dive./*Ullstein*

Below: A fine view of a Ju87R showing the starboard fuel tank clearly./*IWM*

pilot could more easily follow the diversionary action of the target.

In a Staffeln attack against a heavy warship, the formation would close up, shortly before the target was reached, into a tight defensive group, but this would still be based on its original Kette spacing. Once the flight commander had identified the target the Staffel would move up into an echelon formation preparatory to the actual dive.

When about to attack, the formation leader would waggle his wings as a signal, whereupon bombing instruments would be switched on by the other pilots and they would follow the leader down. Cockpit drill at the commencement of a dive would be:

Close radiator flap
Turn off supercharger
Tip over
Set angle of dive
Accelerate
Apply dive brakes

The usual angle of dive was about 70–85 degrees, but the Stukas often went in almost vertically. There were two methods of commencing a dive-bombing attack, either simply pushing the stick forward and going over nose down or, as described above, the peel-off. Here the pilot would half-roll his aircraft on its back and pull the stick hard back. When the nose dropped he would push forward as the sights came on, final corrections being made by individual pilots as they dropped down on the target.

To facilitate aiming during the dive, a series of red marked lines of various angles, like a protractor, was engraved on the cabin side panels, the pilot using these to line-up with the horizon.

On completion of the dive, the pilot had to retract the air-brakes, readjust the bomb-release switches and throttle back, reopening the radiator shutter to stop the engine over-heating. For the Stuka this was the moment of supreme vulnerability and Allied fighters were quick to learn this. Fighters would welcome the opportunity to pounce on Stukas at sea-level with the pilot fully occupied and with no room to manoeuvre, and this led to an early request that against fighter-defended targets, the Stukas' own fighter escort should dive with them to be on hand at this precise moment. This proved to be very unpopular with the fighter pilots who found themselves in a similar position and were soon requesting additional high-cover for themselves.

In theory, anti-aircraft gunners presented with a steeply diving aircraft approaching them head-on, were given an ideal set-shot with no deflection. In practice it needed an extremely hardened gunner to stand his

ground as the evil gull-winged shape grew ever larger in his sights, the bomb dropping away seemingly aimed directly at him and the dreaded high-pitched scream sounding in his ears like his personal death-knell.

It was not until the advent of the fast-firing light automatic weapons, like the Bofors, that the ships could fight back on anything like equal terms.

It was the same ashore. Gen Sir Frederick Pile wrote:
'The Germans and Italians (and the Philippinos under Gen MacArthur), were all prepared to fight without air support. But in the case of our troops, if they were not supported by superior air forces, or if a few dive-bombers attacked them, it was considered unfair, and a "withdrawal to a previously prepared position" was ordered.'*

The bulk of the Stuka force which smashed its way swiftly through Europe in the summer of 1940 was equipped with the Ju87B2, which differed from the B in small refinements such as hydraulically-operated cooling gills on the radiator, an improved broad-bladed airscrew and ejector exhausts. But just coming into service at that time was the Ju87R1, which was a derivative of the B series and identical to the B1 except that it was fitted with attachments for the fitting at short notice of two external fuel tanks under the wings in place of the fragmentation bombs, and the internal fuel tanks were also modified, giving it a range of 875 miles with one 550lb bomb. The 87R (R standing for Reichweit, or Range) was primarily intended for anti-shipping operations and the first unit to use it in combat was 2/StG1 at Stavanger, Norway. I/StG1 was fully equipped when operating under Fliegerkorps VIII in France, the following June. The external fuel tanks could carry 300 litres of fuel on the wing-racks, while the modification to the internal tanks consisted of replacing the metal tanks with fabric ones which would expand outward into the wing crevices, giving additional capacity.

However, on completion of Western operations a new version of the Stuka began to come off the production lines, this being the Ju87D which first appeared in 1940. In this version the oil cooler was removed from its position on top of the cowling and positioned under the cowling in place of the coolant radiator. This, in turn, was re-positioned under the centre wing section and this re-arrangement resulted in an improved engine cowling line. The cockpit was streamlined by fairing the after section downwards and the gunner was given improved defensive cap-

*Gen Sir Frederick Pile; *Ack-Ack*; Harrap, London.

83

ability by the replacement of the single MG15 gun by the twin MG81z.

Fitting the Jumo 211J engine with an induction cooler gave the 87D 1,300hp which meant that a maximum bomb-load of 4,000lb could now be lifted or a combination of two 1,100lb bombs and fragmentation weapons. As a lesson from the Battle of Britain, improved crew protection was fitted which included 8mm plating behind the pilot with 4mm at the sides, an armoured headshield of 10mm plating, and 5mm protection head and sides for the gunner. Performance was 255mph at 13,500ft. The Ju87D1 first featured largely in the initial operations against the Russians in June 1941.

The D2 was a glider tug employed for towing cargo-gliders, chiefly in the Middle East, and only a few were built ,the only modification from the basic D type being a strengthened tail-wheel leg. Freidrich Lang recalls his unit's experience with these cargo gliders on a trip to the Eastern Front thus: 'The I/StG2 received, in May/June 1942, some 15 of these Lastenseglern, DFS230, for use. When at the Graz/Thalerhof airfield where we had been sent to freshen up after the first Russian winter, we practised towing them, so were familiar with the problems.

'The Ju87s allocated for towing were fitted with a new hook arrangement and a simple lever release. I was given the far from easy task of leading the towing formation, Schleppverband, which consisted of 15 Ju87s each with a glider in tow, from Graz via Bruno, Krakov, Lemberg, Schitomir, Konotop to the airfield at Ochotschewka, northeast of Kursk, from where we then started the June offensive towards Woronesch. The Lastensegler were not altogether successful. Too many of them came adrift while being towed and still lay somewhere in the countryside with their loads inside them. Recovery was time-consuming and very difficult.'

However, losses from small-arms fire on the Eastern Front led to a demand from the Stuka crews on ground-attack missions for even more protection, and this led to the introduction, in late 1941, of the D3.

In addition to heavier armouring around the crew, the ground-strafing technique had proven itself invaluable in knocking out the super-heavy Soviet tanks which were impregnable to many of the Wehrmacht anti-tank guns. The D3 therefore carried a wing-mounted tank-busting armament of two MG151 20mm cannon.

For it is a fact that knocking tanks out with bombs proved to be a very difficult operation. On one instance, on the fourth day of operations against Russia, Hauptmann Hitschold led the whole of StG2 in to attack a concentration of about 60 tanks in the area 80km south of Grodno. The bombs fell squarely on the target, but later it was found that only a single tank was knocked out, and this was by machine gun fire from Hitschold's own aircraft. The Soviet type of tank was far less vulnerable to bomb blast effects than the British or French types had been.

Thus it was that the advent of the cannon-firing Stukas was a major step forward, and Rudel and others soon showed what a handy weapon this could be. Alternate weapon packs included a WB81 weapons container under each wing, each of which carried six to eight MG81 machine guns. This fearsome weapon was known as the 'watering can', and with all 12 machine guns fixed to fire forwards and backwards down to the ground, the Stukas quite literally sprayed fire through the Communist troop concentrations with a wide field of fire, causing heavy casualties among their bunched-up infantry formations.

Most of Germany's Allies were forced to acknowledge the superiority of her weapons over anything which they could produce in their own armouries, and as the war progressed they came more and more to rely on her to keep them supplied. In line with this the Stuka was supplied and used extensively. On the Eastern Front it was in use with the air contingents of Rumania, Bulgaria and Hungary and the Slovak Air Force, all of whom took deliveries of the Ju87B and '87D in 1941–42.

Italy, as has been related, took deliveries of several batches of Stukas, and, renamed the 'Picchiatello', they equipped half a dozen Squadriglia and were much in evidence flying against British convoys in the Mediterranean in 1942, where they were invariably reported as German, despite the Fasces markings. Although it was strongly reported at the time that the Societa Italiana Ernesto Breda was manufacturing the Ju87 under licence as the Ba201, this was not the case and all Italian Stukas were supplied by Germany.

In fact as the war went on, more, not less uses were found for the Ju87 on all fronts. Far from being written off, production actually increased from year to year. When in 1942 the Me210 failed to appear as its replacement, the Ju87 received another boost. Despite the fact that RAF pundits had written off the Stukas in August 1940, the production figures tell a very different story.

In 1939, 143 Ju87s rollod off the assembly line. In 1940 – 603; 1941 – 500; 1942 – 960 and by the end of 1943 – 1,672. The bulk of these machines were desperately needed in grim campaigns on the Eastern Front, and we must now retrace our steps to mid-1941 to follow the varying fortunes of the Stukas in that dreadful area.

8 Smashing the Soviets

Hitler had always laid down that the basic policy of the new Reich was the expansion of her territories eastward and had long nursed a hatred for Communism. In the first years of power, while Germany was still weak, it was Stalin who had most actively striven to unite the European powers against Germany, and it was only through the need to secure his flanks that Hitler had been forced to sign a non-aggression pact with Soviet Russia in 1939. Since then he had been forced to endure several humiliations at the hands of his erstwhile ally; the rape of the Baltic States, which had been created originally by German feats of arms in 1918; the invasion of Germany's old friend Finland without any provocation; the division of Poland after German troops had done all the fighting; all these served to increase the determination of the Führer for revenge and a final settlement with Russia.

Cynically Stalin was building up his strength and already the Soviet Army was the largest in the world. While the rest of Europe was engaged in combat, Stalin was quite happy to wait until both sides were exhausted before moving in to pick up the pieces. As it was, the speed and efficiency of the German armed forces cleared Western Europe before the rebuilding of Russian power, shattered at the top by the purges of the late 1930s, had been completed. Despite repeated warnings from his own intelligence and alerts from British and American sources, Stalin was certain that Hitler would not strike at Russia,

In fact as early as the autumn of 1940 Hitler had informed his top military advisers that he intended to move against Russia, and preparations were being made while the Battle of Britain was still in progress. Hitler had never wanted to fight a long war against Great

Below: The Russian campaign opened in June 1941, and the combination of Stuka and Panzer were once more initially irresistible. A Kette of Stukas swoops low over an armoured column during the initial advance./*Ullstein*

Britain and hoped that, after his spectacular victories, she would come to an agreement with Germany which would leave the British Empire intact and leave Hitler a free hand in Europe. It was not to be and the continued belligerence of Britain led to further complications in the Mediterranean.

The campaigns in Jugoslavia, Greece and Crete further delayed the German plan for offensive in the east but by June 1941 she was ready to strike. An army of unprecedented strength and power, with massive supporting air forces, was secretly and carefully moved up all along the 1,000-mile frontier, a redeployment which, although not completely unnoticed by Stalin's aides, Russia chose to ignore.

Jumping-off date for the great offensive was finally fixed for 22 June, by which time Germany and her allies had amassed a force of 3,000,000 men, 600,000 vehicles, 3,580 armoured vehicles and 7,184 guns against the Russian Front. Even this huge concentration was not enough to ensure positive victory, for the Soviet armies facing them totalled some 4,500,000 men, or half as large again, hardly a defence force.

But Germany won the race and to spearhead Operation Barbarossa the Germans had similarly redeployed her air power in no less than four Air Fleets and 1,945 aircraft lay ready to launch the most massive Blitzkrieg of them all. As always the Stuka units would be in the van and a total of 290 Ju87s were available for Day One.

The organisation involved in moving these great numbers eastward across Europe was colossal and the utmost secrecy was maintained. It was a task in which the Luftwaffe excelled and was an outstanding achievement.

Immediately after the end of the Crete campaign von Richthofen's Fliegerkorps VIII was moved through to Poland via Germany, and as early as 1 June the flying units were entraining in Rumania for re-equipping and rest in Germany while their ground support teams proceeded directly to advance bases in Poland. This was all complete in three weeks despite the most difficult lines of communication. At the same time Luftflotte 2 and Fliegerkorps II and V were transferred from France with similar speed.

Stuka Gruppen were distributed ready for the assault. All units were massed under Luftflotte 2, commanded by Kesselring, whose task it was to blast the way open for General-feldmarschall Bock's Army Group Centre which was to penetrate the whole area between Romintener Heides, south of Memel, to Brest-Litovsk, a line of 250 miles. von Bock's command contained two armies and the 2nd Panzer Group led by the famous tank general, Guderian, and the 3rd Panzer Group under

Left: The lean hungry profile of the Junkers Ju87D. /*Franz Selinger*

Centre left: Armourers at work at a Stuka base during the summer months of the 1942 campaign in Russia./*Ullstein*

Bottom left: A Junkers Ju87 'Dora', fresh off the line./*Radinger*

Right: Note the small propellers of the 'Trombones of Jericho' fittings in this head-on shot of a Ju87D. /*Archiv Schliephake*

Below: Head on view of prop and chin intake, the dive brakes can also be seen to good effect./*IWM*

Hoth. Their immediate objective was the annihilation of the enormous Soviet Army concentrations centring on the fortress city of Brest and the area around Smolensk.

Bruno Loerzer's II Air Corps contained StG77 and von Richthofen's VIII Air Corps had the well-tried elements of StG1 and StG2 to open the offensive. Remote from the main front in northern Norway was IV(Stuka)/LG1 designed to take the vital Arctic ports of Murmansk and Archangel. They were under the command of Fliegerführer Kirkenes, part of Luftflotte 5 under Stumpff.

Before dawn on 22 June these forces were airborne to launch the greatest land battle in the history of warfare.

The initial assault exceeded the Germans' wildest hopes, and everywhere the bombers and dive-bombers and strafing fighters swarmed over Soviet airfields to find row upon row of enemy aircraft lined up as if on display; the carnage was terrible. The Russians later admitted that complete surprise was achieved and that on the first day alone they lost the staggering total of 1,800 aircraft for a German loss of 35. This day's fighting was the greatest victory ever achieved by one air force over another. Over 700 of these were destroyed by Kesselring's forces and the Stuka units played a full part.

StG77 first mission was against Soviet defence works along the line of the River Bug, where, thanks to their support, and by the ingenious use of underwater tanks, the 17th and 18th Panzer Divisions were soon across and racing towards Minsk and Smolensk. Meanwhile, Guderian had to reduce the fortress citadel of Brest-Litovsk, which was held by fanatically fierce troops of five Soviet regiments. The Panzers raced on but the Russians inflicted heavy casualties on the German infantry, although one by one the various strong points were mopped up. On the 29th StG1 was sent in to smash one of the forts and its attack was followed up by the Ju88s of

KG3 dropping 4,000lb bombs to shatter the strong walls. By the 30th the fortress had fallen.

Two days later the first great encirclement battle was completed, the two armoured pincers of Hoth and Guderian with their Stuka tips closed on the vast Minsk pocket. Inside this noose were trapped four Soviet armies and they were annihilated. Russian losses were enormous, 32 infantry, cavalry and armoured divisions were smashed and 2,400 tanks, 1,400 guns and 240 aircraft were destroyed or captured.

The swift advances were accompanied by almost daily leaps forward by the ground organisations supporting the short-range Stukas. StG1, for example, had its I and II Gruppen moved forward 360 miles in the first month of operations:

'We stay for short periods at Ulla, Lepel and Janowici. Our targets are always the same: tanks, motor vehicles, bridges, fieldworks and AA sites. On and off our objectives are the enemy's railway communications or an armoured train when the Soviets bring one up to support their artillery. All resistance in front of our spearheads has to be broken so as to increase the speed and impetus of our advance.'*

Towards the end of July Fliegerkorps VII was switched from the Central front to the northern zone of operations to reinforce the drive on Leningrad. Despite the size of the Luftwaffe forces, Russia was so vast that commands had constantly to be switched from one end of the massive front to the other. At Kronstadt in the Baltic lay the Soviet fleet, which consisted of two ancient battleships dating from World War I, whose 12in

*Hans-Ulrich Rudel; *Stuka Pilot*; Euphorion, Dublin.

88

guns were proving a hazard to the German forces advancing on Leningrad itself. In order to silence this troublesome duo, which lay immune from naval assault behind several minefields, the Stukas were to be called in.

The Russians had been forced back to their defensive perimeter around the city and on 8 September the Germans launched their assault which was planned to take Leningrad. However, the Soviets were well dug in and resistance was tough. Stuka units were active over the front and were instrumental in forcing the breakthrough of the first Russian line by the 118th Infantry Regiment which took Apropakosi. On the 11th another assault took place by the 1st Panzer Division against enemy fortified positions in the Duderhof hills to the south of the city. Again close liaison between the Panzers and the Stukas carried the day.

'It was a thrilling spectacle. Above the battalion's spearhead, as it raced forward, roared the Stukas of VIII Air Corps. They banked and accurately dropped their bombs 200 to 300yd in front of the battalion's leading tanks, right on top of the Russian strongpoints, dugouts, ditches, tank-traps and anti-tank guns.

'Luftwaffe liaison officers were in the tanks and armoured infantry carriers of the spearhead and also with the commander of the armoured infantry carrier battalion. A Luftwaffe signals officer, sitting behind the turret of Stove's tank No 611, maintained radio contact with the Stukas. A large Armed Forces pennant on the tank's stern clearly identified him as the "master bomber". In the thick of enemy fire the Luftwaffe Leutnant directed the Stuka pilots through his throat microphone.'*

*Paul Cavell; *Hitler's War on Russia*; Harrap, London.

On the 12th again it was a last-minute intervention by the dive-bombers which effectively broke up a counter-attack by Soviet tank forces, which included the superb T-34s which were impervious to German anti-tank shells. But on the seaward flank of the advancing German divisions the Russians had retained a bridgehead, the Oranienbaum pocket, which contained 12 Soviet divisions, and gunfire from the two battleships and supporting cruisers from the Kronstadt naval base across the water was proving a hazard, especially to the 58th Infantry division.

Accordingly Kesselring sent in, day after day, for almost a week, wave after wave of Stukas to silence the great naval guns. The target was not an easy one like the British fleet off Crete, for the Russians had enmeshed their base with a bristling circle of anti-aircraft guns and these, supplemented by the warships' own AA weapons, turned the skies over Kronstadt into an inferno.

StG2, led by Oskar Dinort – the 'Immelmann' Geschwader, with its unique ship-destroying record – was the unit chosen to lead in this difficult task. Flying with this crack unit was Hans-Ulrich Rudel, a young Stuka pilot soon to make his mark and destined to become famous as one of the Soviet Union's most feared opponents. The first mission with 30 Ju87s took place on 16 September against the battleship *Marat*, which was sighted taking up a bombardment position in the deep water channel between Kronstadt island and Leningrad. It was known that to sink battleships, even old ones, would probably need a heavier missile than the 1,100lb bombs which had so battered the *Illustrious* and other thin-skinned warships, but the 2,000lb bombs being prepared were not yet available so the Stukas were sent out to do what they could against the fire-belching colossus.

Above: A 'Dora' and crew in the Russian wastes, note the mottled paint scheme utilised in these conditions.
/*Archiv Schliephake*

89

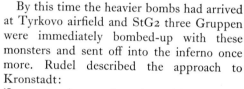

Right: Oberst Dr Ernst Kupfer, here seen with the traditional Jolanthe mascot on achieving his 400th Stuka mission. The Kommodore of StG2, he was appointed the first Waffengeneral der Schlachtflieger in 1943, but was killed in a flying accident in November of the same year. /*Ullstein*

Below: 4th Staffel II/StG77 in the Kuban/Kvymskaja area on 9 March 1942. Wolfinger receives a celebration bouquet. /*Wolfinger via Archiv Schliephake*

Bottom: 4/StG77 over the Djeproprebrowsk Bridge. Note that the wheel 'spats' have been removed to help cope with 'General Mud' on the primitive airstrips of the region. /*Wolfinger via Archiv Schliephake*

Thick cloud with a 2,400ft base made the Gruppe's approach difficult, and as the Stukas were not fitted for blind flying the run up to the target area had to be entrusted to the leader using only the rudimentary ball, bank indicator and vertical speed indicator, while the rest of the aircraft followed him as close as they could.

Nevertheless the commander of III/StG2, Haupt Steen, successfully located the battleship and with his wingman Haupt Klaus, tipped over and commenced the attack. Surprise was achieved and before the ship's ack-ack fire could home on to the gap in the clouds the Ju87s had plummeted through, scoring one direct hit and several near-misses on their target, without loss to themselves. As expected, however, the 1,100lb bomb which hit her failed to sink the *Marat* and some time later she was spotted repairing at Kronstadt.

By this time the heavier bombs had arrived at Tyrkovo airfield and StG2 three Gruppen were immediately bombed-up with these monsters and sent off into the inferno once more. Rudel described the approach to Kronstadt:

'I never again experienced anything to compare with it in any place or theatre of war. The concentrated zones of flak in the air space began as soon as we cross the coastal strip which is still in Soviet hands. Then comes Oranienbaum and Peterhof; being harbours, very strongly defended. The open water is alive with pontoons, barges, boats and tiny craft all stiff with flak. The Russians use every possible site for their AA guns. After about six miles we sight the island of Kronstadt with its great naval harbour and the town of the same name. Both harbour and town are heavily defended, and besides the whole Russian Baltic fleet is anchored in the immediate vicinity in and outside the harbour. And it can put up a murderous barrage of flak.'*

Despite the difficulties the Geschwader pressed on and approaching from 15,000ft located the *Marat* and other heavy ships. All the Stukas pressed on down and at 1,000ft the 2,000lb missiles were released, scoring two direct hits on the battleship which heeled over. One of the bombs pierced a magazine and with a huge explosion which sent up a pall of smoke 1,200ft into the air, the great ship was torn in half.

Even with the destruction of one battleship the attacks were continued and efforts were made to finish off the second, the *Oktobrescaja*

*Hans-Ulrich Rudel; *Stuka Pilot*; Euphorion, Dublin.

Revolutia. During these raids one of Russia's newest cruisers, the 9,500 ton *Kirov*, was the target of StG2 and in leading a Gruppe into the attack its commander, Hauptmann Steen, had his green-nosed Ju87 hit heavily by flak at 5,000ft. The shells smashed his rudder but in an attempt to dive his doomed aircraft into the 7·1in cruiser, Steen tried to steer by the ailerons only, but he missed and thundered into the sea close alongside. His bomb, released moments earlier, crashed into the *Kirov* and severely damaged her. Taking part also in these operations against the Soviet fleet was Staffelkapitän Lehmann, and, as he describes, not all the hazards and dangers of these missions came from the enemy!

'In action the Ju87 was able to fly and land despite the greatest damage. Over the bay of Kronstadt during the operations against the Russian Baltic Fleet, I was hit by a 4cm flak-grenade in the wing, which punched straight through it, leaving a hole like a Tulip Head. This had no effect whatsoever on the flying ability of my Ju87, and I got safely back to base without any trouble.

'On another mission in the same area, a young pilot who was in action for the first time, dropped his bombs too early during his power dive. Since he was diving immediately behind my machine, one of his 50kg bombs dropped through my wing, close to the fuselage, since, at the moment of impact, I myself had flattened out at the end of my attack pattern. Apart from a hole in the wing, the bomb had pierced one side of the aileron bar and the landing flap, but, despite this, I was able to fly home and even made a good landing.

'In the latter condition it would be apt to point out that another excellent character-istic of the Ju87 was its low starting and landing speed. A firm field or a dry meadow 2-300m in length and 30-50m width, was more than sufficient to take-off and land in.

'Thus, when on a sortie in hostile hinter-land, if a Ju87 was forced to land with damage, or the failure of the engine, it was only necessary to find a landing area of the above dimensions for a forced landing. One comrade of my squadron landed there as well, took on the pilot of the damaged plane, with his wireless operator, and started to fly back to the air base with the rescued crew. My radio operator and I have been rescued like this in Russia and a lot of other crews as well simply because of the ability of the Ju87 to operate thus.'

Before the attacks could be resumed the whole Geschwader received orders to pack up and shift base again, this time it hurried far to the south where another huge battle of encirclement was raging.

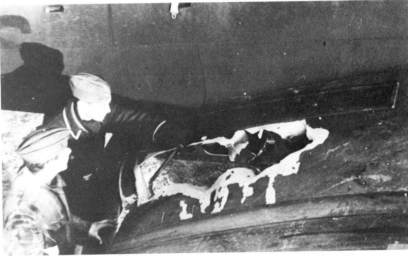

Above: Stuka toughness. It was inevitable that close support missions should lay the dive-bombers open to ground fire, which grew more intense as the war went on. Luckily the Ju87 was an extremely tough and durable little aircraft, as many testiments show, and could survive ghastly damage and return intact./*Lehmann*

Right: Tragschlepp – A Ju87 lifted by an He111 Towmaster for supply missions. */Archiv Schliephake*

Below: WB81 weapons container pack with six Mk81 MGs for spraying Soviet infantry concentrations. */Archiv Schliephake*

Bottom: MG81Z fitted in the rear of the cockpit for this Stuka's defence. */Archiv Schliephake*

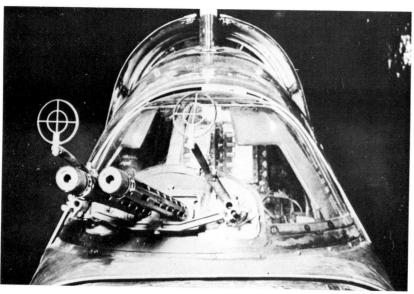

Following the first month's breathtaking advances across eastern Poland and the deep penetrations into the vastness of Russia itself, the German High Command had wished to punch straight on and take Moscow, hub of the Russian communications network, before winter set in. Others, dazzled by the immense casualties they had already inflicted, felt that one more large-scale battle of annihilation would break the Soviet armies and it was to this view that Hitler gave his support.

The orders given to the Panzer armies were not to take Moscow, a mere 200 miles away, and seemingly wide-open, but to drive southwards towards Kiev, forcing the Dnieper river line taking the Soviet 5th Army in the rear. Once this was achieved the oil and great wheat-producing areas of the south-east basin would fall into Germany's pocket. Most of the German generals were appalled at this decision and Guderian even flew home to try and persuade Hitler to change his mind, but the Führer remained adamant.

Therefore Army Groups Centre and South commenced their campaign, both of which proved successful. After much hard fighting, Kleist's Panzers trapped and wiped out three Russian armies between Kiev and Odessa in the battle of Uman. Meantime, Stalin had told his forces to hold fast to the bend of the River Dnieper in front of Kiev no matter what. This was the Germans' opportunity, and supported by waves of Stukas the 4th Panzer Division hurtled down from the north on September 9th and five days later the First and Second Panzer Groups linked up, after punching from the north and south, 130 miles *east* of Kiev. Within their steel claws lay 50

Russian divisions. Heavy fighting continued as the encircled Soviets sought to break free and the dive-bombers were constantly in action, but, by 26 September, it was all over. Five Communist armies, 1,000,000 men, had been wiped out. Small wonder that Hitler was convinced that the Russians were finished. But the victory, although immense, was to cost the Germans a vital month, a month in which the onset of the feared Russian winter was to end their dream of Moscow by Christmas forever.

For now that the way to the Ukraine was forced open, Hitler finally agreed that the Russian capital should be the next objective and the Stuka squadrons were yet again switched several hundreds of miles north and south to take part in this probe. Code-named Typhoon it was to be launched on 2 October and would be, according to the Führer, 'The last great decisive battle of the year'.

In fact the German armies moved off three days earlier, on 30 September, and the great double battle of Vyazma-Bryansk developed. It lasted for a month and at the finish yet another incredible victory had been won. Nine Russian armies had been surrounded and defeated and enormous quantities of arms and supplies taken. More, the road to Moscow was wide open. Why then did the Germans fail to take it? It was simply that no matter what they did against the Soviet forces, they were simply not prepared for a winter campaign and when it came the Panzers and Stukas bogged down all along the line.

If the Germans were ill-prepared for a winter slugging match in the mud and the snow then the Russians found themselves in

their element, and to the north of Moscow, at Kalinin, fresh Siberian divisions put in attack after attack against German bridgeheads. It was only non-stop flights by Richthofen's faithful Stuka units against Russian tank concentrations which prevented a rout.

The Germans had fought their way to within five miles of the Kremlin but they were destined to get no further. In the south also the Ju87s were used to blast open Russian defences, forts and gun emplacements for the opening of the first battle for Sevastopol on 17 December, but here again the effort required proved just too much for them and the fortress held out. Leningrad, Moscow and Sevastopol, everywhere in that bitter winter of 1941 the German assaults ground to a halt just short of their targets, defeated by Generals 'Mud' and 'Winter'.

Lack of suitable equipment for servicing and maintaining their aircraft meant that in some Stuka units serviceable aircraft fell to less than 30%. III/StG2, for example, had fallen back on Rhew and conditions here were typical. Engines would not start, everything froze stiff as temperatures plummeted to −20°F. Mechanics were out all night warming up the engines at half-hour intervals to prevent them freezing up solid, and many men went down with frostbite.

In the midst of the desolation and misery the Russians launched their counter-offensive which was held with only the greatest difficulty and self-sacrifice. Also during the winter, Fliegerkorps II was pulled out and transferred to the Mediterranean, leaving the Stukas of Fliegerkorps VIII to hold the central front alone.

Far up north beyond the Arctic Circle the whine of the Stuka had also been heard. Gen Dietl, 'Hero of Narvik', had been ordered to cooperate with Finnish forces and launch an attack to sever communications between Murmansk and southern Russia by cutting the railway line. It was futher hoped to take and destroy the White Sea ports to prevent the Soviets from launching a strike at Hitler's vital nickel mines at Petsamo, a bare 60 miles away.

Code-named Platinum Fox, the 2nd and 3rd Mountain Divisions under Dietl launched their initial assault on 22 June and struck out to the east. On the 24th they had sealed off Rybachiy Peninsula and bypassed the Russian fortifications and armoured pill-boxes along the Finnish frontier. Strikes by IV(Stuka)/LG1 later pulverised these strongpoints in their rear. This Gruppe was also instrumental in destroying the bulk of the Russian fighter defences which it bombed and shot up at the Murmansk airfields, destroying over 100 machines.

Even so, the northern tundra proved to be impossible terrain to fight in, being trackless. The Stukas were withdrawn and sent further south to attack positions around Salla and despite further penetrations, after laborious preparation, during which the 3rd Mountain Division took Litsa, they were still 27 impossible miles from Murmansk.

The Stukas forced the way through Salla and the Finnish forces, reinforced by German elements, pressed on towards their objective, Kandalaksha on the Murmansk-Moscow railway, 250 miles south of the port, but they in turn became snowed down short of their objective. Fresh Siberian divisions launched counter-attacks and by the end of the September fighting the front line had become stabilised. Murmansk remained free and through it would pour an ever increasing flood of American war material to rebuild and reinforce the shattered Soviet armies.

But while the dive-bombers waged unceasing battle in the snow, frost, slush and mud of the endless Russian plain, further south their comrades were equally fully extended throughout the length and breadth of the Eastern Mediterranean and in the hot dry deserts of Libya and Egypt.

Top right: Hand-fuelling a 1/StG2 Stuka. /*Hans Obert*

Centre right: Preparing for a sortie-note the 'Trombones of Jericho' on wheel legs. /*Hans Obert*

Right: Scottie Dog symbol of I Gruppe. Yellow background indicates of 3 Staffel./*Hans Obert*

9 Bane of the Convoys

The Mediterranean operations, which took place between 1941 and 1942, can be summarised as having three main sections. The maintenance of the island of Malta as a striking base against Axis sea communications in the Central Mediterranean which led to a series of hard fought convoy actions, each of which became more and more bitterly contested, was the first section. Convoys were sailed either via the Straits of Gibraltar in the west, when Force H acted as their guardians, or else came around the Cape and were fought through from Alexandria with the main Mediterranean Fleet providing the protection. Both routes were hazardous in the extreme and the condition of the fleet and the size of the enemy forces were both instrumental in deciding the success or failure of these convoys.

Secondly the various offensives and counter-offensives in the desert campaign, as the Axis sought to thrust through to the Suez Canal and the British attempted first to contain them and then to counter-attack, made for a ding-dong series of intensive land operations up and down the coast, and the investment of Tobruk early in 1941 added additional burdens to both defender and attacker alike. To the British the garrison was a drain on their limited resources, as shipping had to run the gauntlet with supplies and suffered heavily. But it was an attractive prestige operation from Churchill's point of view. The Axis was ever conscious of this base in its rear and expended considerable effort to neutralise it.

The third section can be seen as the Axis attempts to eliminate Malta by concentrated bombing offensives. Again the scale of effort, although almost continuous, varied according to strategic situations on other fronts and on the availability of Luftwaffe units in sufficient numbers. In all these sections of the complex war in the Mediterranean, the Stuka dive-bomber featured prominently.

As has been recorded, the Germans were now slow in providing their Italian ally with large quantities of Ju87s and in Italian hands it proved itself no less a weapon than before. A dive-bombing leaders' school was established at Foggia under Oberst Peltz and rapidly expanded. One of the first Italian Stuka formations to be established and equipped was 239 Squadriagle which was deployed in the North African campaign early in May 1941. While the German Stuka *Gruppen* were heavily engaged in the Crete campaign and winning new laurels there, 239 was proving itself with its new aircraft off Libya.

This unit, never more than 10 aircraft strong, was early into action against ship targets in the Tobruk area, and concentrated almost exclusively on disrupting supplies to that garrison. Its first victory was achieved on

Below: The Greek Front. Battle formation for Junkers Ju87B-2s of 208 Squadriglia of 101° Gruppo Autonomo B. at T. returning to their base after striking at enemy airfields. */AMI via N. Malizia*

25 May when it caught and sank the supply ship *Hekla* (3,470 ton) in Tobruk harbour, and in the same raid the sloop *Grimsby* was caught outside the harbour and sunk.

The following day No 239 Squadriagle attacked shipping at Marsa Luch but failed to score any hits. On 24 June five Stukas from this unit sank the anti-aircraft sloop *Auckland* off Tobruk. She was an Australian vessel of the same type as the *Bittern* sunk at Norway, and five days later 239 scored an even greater success against the Australian Navy.

Adm Cunningham has recorded that the supply of Tobruk was a great drain on destroyers and small ships. Two nights out of three a pair of destroyers would be sent in with stores as a matter of routine and the 'Tobruk Run' gained the same kind of notoriety as the 'Tokyo Express' runs that the Japanese destroyers were later to make to reinforce Guadalcanal – the losses suffered were equally severe.

On one such mission the destroyers *Defender* and *Waterhen* (RAN) slipped out of Alexandria on 28 June laden with supplies and troop reinforcements. Undetected as they sped along the coast and at full readiness for action they had a peaceful passage until they reached the Gulf of Sollum on the evening of the 29th. Hopes were high that with the approach of nightfall they could slip into Tobruk in the

Right: Another strike takes-off for Tobruk, June, 1942. /*Archiv Schliephake*

Below: A Junkers Ju87B of 239 Squadriglia over the rugged terrain of the Libyan desert, 1941./*AMI via N. Malizia*

Bottom: A dusty take-off for this Stuka of 239 Squadriglia in Libya during the early days of 1942./*AMI via N. Malizia*

darkness, unload, and be clear by dawn the following morning.

At 1945hrs these hopes were dashed by the sighting of an approaching formation of aircraft, and, as they arrived overhead, their silhouettes were unmistakably those of Stukas. The two destroyers took the usual violent avoiding action as the Ju87s tipped over and commenced their attacks. Some accounts give the number of Stukas involved as 42 but in fact there were only seven of 239 Squadriagle and they made no mistakes.

The *Waterhen* was hit by a 550lb bomb and holed by splinters from numerous near-misses, although she suffered no casualties. She slid to a halt and the *Defender* came alongside and took off her complement of troops. Then, still under attack, she steamed away. *Waterhen* lay stopped but survived further attack and after dark her companion returned and took her in tow in the hope of saving her, but this was not to be. The ancient little destroyer (she was built for the Grand Fleet in 1918) finally rolled over and sank at 0150.

The *Defender* survived this encounter but was hit in an almost identical air attack on 11 July off Sidi Barrani and foundered in tow of the Australian destroyer *Vampire*. Other kills registered by this proficient Italian unit were the sinking of a steamer off Raz Azzaz on

Left: Junkers Ju87B2s of 101° Gruppo taking off from an airfield in southern Italy for an attack on the Albania front in 1941./*AMI vi N. Malizia*

Below: A large formation of Junkers Ju87/Trop Stukas in desert colour scheme, head out over the desert to apply the coup-de-grace to Tobruk./*IWM*

15 July and attacks on a submarine off Tripoli on the 28th.

Over in the Western Basin the Ju87s of Fliegerkorps X were busy, the *Tiger* convoy from Gibraltar being attacked by them on 8 and 9 May without success. During that month the bulk of this force was transferred to the Balkans and later missions were flown by Italian units, notably by 101 Gruppo based on Sicily.

In the desert Fliegerführer Afrika was supporting Rommel with two Gruppen of Stukas but their strength was never more than 60 aircraft at one time and not all were operational. This unit operated Ju87R2/Trop Stukas, StG1 being especially active early on. (Trop=tropicalised for desert use.) The Italians added the support of one Squadriagle (some 10 to 12 aircraft), initially it was No 239 and later No 209 Squadriagle. In April only 40 of the German Stukas, based around Derna, were operational, with six of the Italians.

With the Luftwaffe heavily engaged in Russia there was a slackening of Stuka operations in the Mediterranean throughout the later months of 1941, the only activity being an abortive raid by nine of 101 Gruppo against Malta convoy 'Substance' on 27 September.

The arrival, late in November, of Kesselring's Luftflotte 2 with Bruno Loerzer's ace Fliegerkorps II, in the Central Mediterranean, heralded a concentration of strength which was to dominate all further operations in the area. Kesselring assumed responsibility for the whole zone and under him II and X Fliegerkorps were assigned to the Central and Eastern areas respectively. Although the planned airborne occupation of Malta was discussed at length it was finally abandoned, due to Hitler's fear that the Italians would not be up to the task and his hope that the Luftwaffe could reduce the island unaided. Meanwhile, a new offensive was to be launched by Rommel and his Italian partners to take the Nile basin.

Fliegerkorps II concentrated two Gruppen and two Staffeln of Stukas at Castelvetrano airfield in Sicily with a total strength of 70 plus Ju87s. By the end of December the German air strength had risen to 425 aircraft of all types and the assault on Malta commenced.

Starting in mid-January, the scale of attack grew to a climax in March and April and the densely packed urban area around the naval harbour of Valetta was pulverised. In the harbour itself, target for the bulk of the Stuka raids, the Royal Navy suffered grievous blows. At the beginning of the assault several cruisers and destroyers were caught at Malta undergoing refits from battle damage received in the hotly contested convoy actions of January and March, but Malta rapidly changed from a haven for these cripples to a death trap.

Losses mounted, reaching their peak in April. Such ships as survived the earlier attacks were patched up and sailed to safety at Gibraltar and Alexandria but many were immobilised and finished off. One day, 5 April, saw the destruction of no less than three destroyers, *Gallant*, *Kingston* and *Lance*, which were all hit and wrecked, while many smaller ships, minesweepers and auxiliaries were sunk. 125 aircraft were destroyed in the equally effective attacks on Malta's airfields, but all this was not achieved without cost to the Luftwaffe. Count Ciano, the Italian Foreign Minister, noted cynically: 'The Germans have lost many feathers over Malta.'

Indeed the Malta defence was far removed from the spare Gloster Gladiator fighters with which she had entered the war. The dockyard was ringed with hundreds of AA guns and frequent reinforcements of Spitfires were ferried in by British carriers, supplemented on two occasions by the USS *Wasp*, which effectively disputed control of the island sky.

On 10 May Kesselring assumed that the battle was won, and indeed, as a naval base for surface ships Malta had certainly been neutralised, but submarines and torpedo-bombers kept operating despite the difficulties and continued to blast at the Axis shipping

Left: Early in 1942 Kesselring initiated an all-out air assault in order to eliminate Malta as a naval base. Widespread damage was caused and all surface vessels were sunk, damaged or driven from the island. Ju87Ds form up over Sicily to deliver another attack./*Franz Selinger*

Centre left: During the spring Blitz on Malta in 1942 the island was made untenable to major surface warships and several destroyers were crippled or sunk in dock there, one of them being the *Kingston./IWM*

Bottom left: A Junkers Ju87 of 101° Gruppo returning to its Sicilian airbase after another attack on Malta./*N. Malizia*

Above: Stuka over Malta during the prolonged blitz of 1942. /*Archiv Schliephake*

Left: The CO of a desert Stuka unit briefs his men for yet another mission against the Eighth Army./*IWM*

routes. Meanwhile, many units, including II/StG3, were transferred to North Africa to aid Rommel in his new offensive, which began on 26 May.

A very vivid account of what it is like to be on the receiving end of a Stuka attack is given by Mr Rowlands:

'During the week prior to 1 June 1942, the 7th Medium Regiment, Royal Artillery, was attached to the 150th Brigade and we were before Gazala in what had become known to the troops as "Stuka Alley". The Stukas came every morning with a regularity that you could set your watch by, and for us on the ground it was a waiting game to see who would be the next to be attacked by them.

'Our turn came on 1 June, we have been towed in to some gun pits from which a 25 pounder battery had been shelled out. A similar fate was soon to overtake us. We were then towed by tanks to take up position on the open desert, the terrain being very rocky, and it was impossible to dig gun pits or slit-trenches.

'It was about 1000hrs and we were in action against German armour. The noise from the gunfire and counter-shelling on our position was shattering, and it was only when I happened to glance up that I realised the dive-bombers were already circling overhead. "This is it", I thought, and flung myself to the ground as all hell broke loose. My gun was soon hit and I remember being lifted up and crashing to the ground time and time again as the explosions rocked our position.

'When the smoke and dust cleared, the guns

and transport were a mass of tangled metal and fire, with ammunition exploding around. After a time I felt pain from head to toe. I had no wounds but had extensive bruising from bouncing on the grass. Casualties were heavy, but we were soon over-run and I was taken prisoner. The relief was sweet – I never wanted to experience dive-bombing again.'*

Cutting round in a wide sweep the Afrika Korps outflanked the British position at Gazala and heavy Stuka attacks mounted by StG3, led by General-leutnant Sigel, reduced the strong points of the defensive system in heavy attacks on 3 June. Despite this, much heavy fighting developed around the defences at Bir Hacheim, StG3 losing 14 aircraft in one week's fighting.

Peak strength of the dive-bomber forces reached 70 machines during this period and this was maintained despite heavy losses and an intensive sortie ratio achieved by the Stukas, who mounted 100 attacks during the first week of the offensive alone. In order to break the Bir Hacheim position the Germans concentrated their entire Stuka strength and on 9 June over 100 Ju87s, in two waves, were sent in against the French division holding this key position. Not surprisingly, after two days' follow-up assault by German infantry, the fortress fell.

Rommel was now through and the British retreat became a rout. Tobruk, which had held out so long the year before, was taken by surprise attack after being by-passed by the speeding Axis formations. The whole operation was a model of Panzer/Stuka cooperation. StG3 pulverised the defences in a dawn attack at 0502hrs and the German infantry

streamed through. Further air attacks by Ju88 Bf110 and Cr42 formations culminated in another heavy Stuka raid on the Pilastrino and Solaro forts in which the Italian 209 Squadriagle with 10 machines participated. Tobruk fell in 24 hours.

By the end of August the British were bundled back to the El Alamein position and Rommel paused, gathering his resources for the knock-out blow. Despite three years of intensive activity the Stuka still, in 1942, retained its ability to create panic and confusion in the enemy infantry units. Alan Moorehead wrote:
'Apart from a few improvised fighters we had no dive-bombers at all. It is useless for military strategists to argue, as they will and fiercely, that the Stuka is a failure and very vulnerable. Ask the troops in the field. Its effect on morale alone made it worth while in the Middle East as long as we had insufficient fighters. Anyway, we thought it good enough to attempt to evolve a dive-bomber of our own.'*

And it was not only morale which justified the Stukas as the loss of Tobruk has shown. Also during this advance, at a most critical moment, both Gens Briggs and Lumsden were wounded by shrapnel from a Stuka bomb in the desert.

While Kesselring wrote of the offensive: 'Weak as were the German-Italian air forces in Africa, they were yet superior to the British. German fighters controlled the battle areas, the British dread of the Stukas equalling our men's affection for them.'†

*Alan Moorehead; *The Desert War*; Hamish Hamilton, London.

†*Kesselring Memoirs*, William Kimber, London.

*Information from Mr. B. de H. Rowlands, February, 1970.

Above left: A Junkers Ju87 of 209 Squadriglia during a short respite in the Libyan desert. Note the primitive state of the strip and the equipment, and the crews goggles and the engine covering./*AMI via N. Malizia*

Above: A Stuka flying over the Cyrenaican coastline, 1941. /*Archiv Schliephake*

It could not last, however, and the cost to the Luftwaffe of the June offensive, coupled with the increasing shortage of fuel oil and the mounting strength of the RAF in the Middle East, meant that Rommel reached the El Alamein position on his last legs. A pause was necessary to replenish but during that pause the tide of victory ebbed from the Axis and passed, finally, to the British.

A large factor in the wastage of the German air strength was the continued demands made on them to destroy the numerous convoys mounted by the Royal Navy to keep Malta on its feet. Each one became a major fleet operation and the indifferent performance of the Italian Fleet meant that a disproportionate amount of the offensive against these convoys had to be borne by units of Luftflotte 2 in addition to their other tasks.

In June the Navy mounted one of the largest operations – convoys sailing from both ends of the Mediterranean in an effort to split the Axis forces available to attack them. From Gibraltar, convoy 'Harpoon', consisting of six storeships and tankers, sailed escorted by the battleship *Malaya*, the old carriers *Eagle* and *Argus*, three modern cruisers and eight destroyers. From Alexandria and Port Said sailed the 'Vigorous' convoy, 11 freighters with an escort of eight cruisers and 27 destroyers commanded by Admiral Vian. Both forces were at sea on 12 June converging on Malta.

Air attacks against the 'Harpoon' convoy commenced on the 14th when the Italian forces based on Sardinia attacked with Cr42 fighter-bombers at 1030hrs, followed by 14 S84 and 18 SM79 torpedo-bombers, 18 Cant Z 1007b medium bombers and 19 Cr42s escorted by 20 C200 fighters. The total number of defending fighters which could be put up from both carriers was only 10 and the defence was swamped. The cruiser *Liverpool*

101

Top: Malta Convoy 'Pedestal': 1/StG3 made a heavy attack on the aircraft carrier *Indomitable* scoring both hits and near misses which put her out of action./*IWM*

Above: Badly damaged and on fire aft, the stricken *Indomitable* hauls out of line while her protecting AA cruiser, *Phoebe*, tries vainly to shield her from further Stuka bombs./*IWM*

was hit by a torpedo and had to be towed to Gibraltar and the freighter *Tanimbar* was sunk by bombs.

It was not until the 15th that the remains of the convoy had come within range of the Stukas and at 0500hrs 17 Ju87s of 102 Gruppo, guided by a SM79 and escorted by 19 C200 fighters, took off from Gela airfield and attacked the ships. They claimed hits on a cruiser and a merchant ship.

Further air raids by Italian and German aircraft, and by units of the Italian Fleet, took place and the convoy was gradually whittled down. At midday 102 Gruppo, with 10 aircraft made a further attack, claiming hits on another two merchant ships, but lost two Stukas to ships' gunfire. Having survived air and surface assault all day, the remains of the convoy ran into a minefield off Malta and lost more ships. In all, only two of the six freighters reached the island.

The 'Vigorous' convoy from the east fared even worse. The main Italian fleet sailed and

placed itself between the convoy and Malta, and while the British awaited the results of air attacks against it, the convoy in turn was subjected to an all-out assault by Luftwaffe formations based on Crete, Greece and Libya.

Several of the merchantmen and escorts developed faults and had to be sent back, and one of these, the Dutch freighter *Aagtekirk*, was caught off Tobruk by II/StG3. Overwhelmed in a mass attack by 40 Stukas the escorting destroyer *Tetcott* fought back bravely and claimed the destruction of three Ju87s, but she was unable to save the merchant ship which went to the bottom under a hail of bombs.

On the 15th and 16th the force of Adm Vian was beset by wave after wave of bomber, E-boat and submarine attacks and by the time it was finally turned back, the cruiser *Hermione* and the destroyers *Airedale*, *Hasty* and *Nestor* had been sunk, the first and last by dive-bombers, as well as two more freighters. The cruiser *Birmingham* had been badly damaged by Stukas. The whole effort had cost the Luftwaffe just one Ju88 and one Ju87 and not a single ship reached Malta.

By far the largest and greatest of the Malta convoy battles of 1942 were the massive attacks launched against the 'Pedestal' convoy of August.*

To oppose this convoy the Axis mustered every serviceable aircraft, and even flew in planes from North Africa and Crete to deal with it. Consisting of 14 large merchant ships, the convoy passed the Straits of Gibraltar on the night of 9/10 August escorted by two battleships, three large carriers, six cruisers, an anti-aircraft cruiser and over 30 destroyers.

*For a complete account of this battle see *Pedestal*; Peter C. Smith; William Kimber, London.

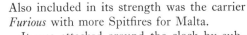

Right: A good air-to-air shot of a Junkers Ju87B2 of 101° Gruppo Note the diving bird symbol on the wheel spat./*N. Malizia*

Below: A fine study of a pair of Junkers Ju87B2s of 208 Squadriglia./*N. Malizia*

Bottom: A Stuka of 208 Squadriglia undergoing maintenance at Trapani Milo airfield./*AMI via N. Malizia*

Also included in its strength was the carrier *Furious* with more Spitfires for Malta.

It was attacked around the clock by submarines, E-boats and aircraft from the 11th until the survivors reached Malta between the 13th and 15th. The Ju87 forces played a large part in the action. The Italians had available some 30 Stukas of 102 Gruppo while the Luftwaffe got ready quickly 26 Stukas of I/StG3 resting at Trapani.

102 Gruppo, operating from Pantelleria, went into the attack with nine bombers at 1840hrs on the 12th after rendezvousing 18 miles NE of Galitia Island. Divided into two sub-flights they planned to synchronise their attack with bomber and torpedo bomber units. Although they pressed home their dives, scoring near-misses on the battleship *Rodney* and the cruiser *Cairo*, they scored no hits and lost two of their number in the process.

The convoy's only casualty to air attack, up until this time, had been one destroyer hit by an aerial torpedo but at this moment 12 Stukas of I/StG3 arrived overhead and, plunging down through an enormous barrage, they scored no less than two direct hits and three very near-misses on the carrier *Indomitable*. Although large fires were started the carrier remained afloat but could not operate her aircraft and turned back. The cost to the dive-bombers was one aircraft torn apart by the inferno of anti-aircraft fire.

During the night the convoy, with a close escort of only cruisers and destroyers, suffered heavy casualties from submarine and E-boat attacks and by dawn on the 13th had become widely dispersed. The Axis air forces then set about mopping up the survivors. At 0915hrs 16 of 102 Gruppo's Stukas bored in on the main group, in what the escorting Admiral described as 'an attack of the most determined nature'. Their target was the vital solitary tanker *Ohio*.

103

One 550lb bomb ploughed into her, but defensive fire from the tanker and the destroyer *Ashanti* hit and destroyed two of the attackers. One Ju87, heavily hit by Oerlikon fire, plummeted straight into the tanker and exploded, but still the *Ohio* remained afloat. Indeed she was one of the five ships which finally arrived at Malta. The comparative success of this convoy lifted the threat of starvation from the island and Malta resumed with renewed vigour her rôle as a base for all types of attack on the Axis supply routes.

The forces assembled to attack 'Pedestal' was the high-water mark of Axis air strength in the Mediterranean theatre. Thereafter it was forced more and more on to the defensive, and, as its strength waned, its losses were not replaced. The open wound of Russia drew away more and more of the Reich's dwindling resources and Allied pressure grew on all sides.

Montgomery opened the final British offensive on the El Alamein front on 24 October and, weak in the air, and overwhelmed by the freshly equipped British armies, Rommel was put to flight. All available aircraft were thrown in to stop the breakthrough, but these were ground under by attrition and by November the Stuka formations supporting the Afrika Korps had been reduced to a mere 30 operational aircraft.

Nor was this their only concern, for on 8 November the Anglo-American forces hit the beaches in French North Africa and, quickly overcoming Vichy resistance, threatened to take the Axis armies in the rear. Although Luftflotte 2 had 30 Stukas based in Sardinia and Sicily at this time they were too few to affect the issue. Most of them were rushed into Tunisia where for a short time, with their backs to the sea, the Luftwaffe gained a period of local air superiority again.

By far the greater strength of the German air forces lay in the squadrons of torpedo and long-range bombers rushed south from France, Norway and even Russia, but even these were not sufficient. The dive-bomber units flown in from Sicily formed part of the striking force of the newly formed Fliegerfuhrer Tunisia, some of them operating from a concrete roadway near the capital which served in lieu of a runway (and indeed in the appalling weather conditions which dominated the campaign that December served them far better than the mud strips of the Allies). By the end of the year there were still only 60 Stukas operating in the Mediterranean, 10 in Sicily, 20 in Tunisia and 30 covering Rommel's retreat westward. The Germans were beginning to rely more and more on the fast fighter-bomber types, Fw190 and Bf110, for ground support, for it was increasingly obvious that command of the air, so essential for the slow Ju87, had been lost.

Even so the Stuka units, operating with the newly introduced Hs129 formations, were instrumental in giving the Allied forces a last bloody nose in the offensives at Feriana and Sbeitla, when they flew 360 sorties on 14 February 1943. But local victories could not affect the major issue and by the end of April all surviving dive-bomber forces had been pulled back to Sicily and the Italian mainland. The writing was clearly on the wall.

Right: A Junkers Ju87R of 103° Gruppo after a forced landing at Ampugnano airport, near Siena, central Italy, in 1943.
/*D. Focarelli via N. Malizia*

10 The Carrier that Never Was

The story of the air-sea cooperation by the German Air Force and Navy is a sorry tale, but one in which the Stuka played a brief part. In its prewar planning the Navy had long schemed to reduce the deficit in battleships *vis-à-vis* the British Navy by building and operating aircraft carriers. It was planned to operate specially converted Ju87s as its chief striking forces, and, had the plan materialised, it promised success, more so once the ship-busting potential of the dive-bomber had shown itself off Norway and the Low Countries. But the plan, after many false starts, finally came to nothing.

Ever since the Luftwaffe had been unveiled and had started its crash programme of expansion, Goering had insisted that 'everything that flies belongs to me', and was highly contemptuous of seaborne aviation in any form. Moreover the Navy, from 1935 onward, was milked of its finest aviators who were summarily transferred to the Air Force. This left the Navy very little to build on but nevertheless it made a start in the 1935 building programme which called for the construction of Germany's first aircraft carrier, to be named *Graf Zeppelin*.

Starting from scratch with, to them, a totally new concept, was a great handicap to the German Navy and the *Graf Zeppelin*'s final design, when revealed, was thought to be faulty by the experts in Great Britain, the United States and Japan. The main fault lay in the fact that the German designers were influenced more by the ship side of her function than by her aerial rôle. With a displacement of 23,200 tons, similar in size to the then current British Illustrious class ships, then under construction, she featured in her defensive armament no less than 16 wholly unnecessary 5·9in low-angled guns for protection against surface vessels. Weapons of this type had been taken to sea by early carriers in all navies, some British ships mounting an 8in calibre weapon, but the new trend of thought was for all armament on carriers to be concentrated on the anti-aircraft rôle, leaving any surface threat to be

Below: The launch of the aircraft carrier *Graf Zeppelin*. Her main striking complement of aircraft was to have consisted of Stukas especially adapted for carrier operations, but the carrier was never completed./*Ullstein*

dealt with by accompanying battleships or cruisers. In any case the 5·9in gun was a light cruiser weapon and would have been totally inadequate against a British heavy cruiser of the County type used to patrol the distant sea lanes. Since it was against these routes that the planned carrier would be required to operate, these guns were merely an added encumbrance and reduced weight and space available to more important functions.

Her anti-aircraft defence, on the other hand, something at which the Germans were far in advance of current British thought in 1939, was very good. The 12 4·1in guns were positioned, somewhat clumsily, along the starboard side and were controlled by four directors. This was the policy of the new Essex class carriers of the United States but such an arrangement was found to be unsatisfactory as it meant restricting the guns' fire arcs to the starboard side only or alternately to stop flying operations while the guns engaged targets to port. The secondary AA armament consisted of 22 37mm and 28 20mm light automatic weapons and was far superior to anything mounted by British warships at that time, and indeed for 10 years afterwards. She had a design speed of 33·75kts which was excellent but her flight deck was armoured with 1·5–2in protection which further encroached on her aircraft stowage, without providing sufficient defence.

Her complement of aircraft was 40, which was very small, and would presumably have been made up of roughly equal numbers of Stukas and fighter aircraft. The ship was launched at Kiel in 1938 and work was started on a sister ship, but thereafter the whole project ran into increasing difficulties.

In exchange for the transfer of men to the Luftwaffe, Goering had promised Grand-

Top: A rare photograph of the Junkers Ju87C, Trägerflugzeug, carrier-borne dive-bomber with wings folded. As well as this feature it had jettisonable undercarriage and an arrestor hook. Naval pilots trained in dive-bombing, but, with the failure of the project, they were absorbed into the Luftwaffe.

Above: Maj Rudel's impressive Stuka combat record in 1944. /*Franz Selinger*

Left: Front view of Maj Rudel's personal Kannonenvogel, 10/StG1./*Franz Selinger*

Admiral Raeder that he would provide, by 1942, all the naval cooperation machines that it required. The estimate in 1935 was for 62 squadrons or about 700 machines. This figure was never remotely approached prewar, and, in practice, despite opposition from the Navy, such units that were provided were soon incorporated back into the Luftwaffe and their tactical commander was only seconded to the Navy for special exercises.

Worse was to come, for in November 1938, with *Graf Zeppelin*'s construction proceeding apace, the Air Force informed the Navy that the Luftwaffe considered itself fully responsible for all air operations over the sea. A period of intense wrangling took place, similar to the controversy of the Fleet Air Arm then reaching its climax in Britain, but in January 1939, when an agreement was finally settled upon, it was the Luftwaffe who held the reins.

The only concessions allowed to Raeder were that the control of air reconnaissance over the sea were to come under the Navy; everything else was Air Force. The Luftwaffe agreed to supply the Navy with nine squadrons of seaplanes, 18 squadrons of medium bombers, 12 carrier-borne squadrons and two squadrons of catapult aircraft for use on heavy ships. The great bulk of the aircraft eventually so designated; six bomber wings were exclusively equipped with Heinkel He 111s, although the new Junkers Ju88 bomber was to form another Gruppe when available. All these were standard medium bomber types equipped with normal armour-piercing bombs. The torpedo was relegated to a few float-plane units only.

For the carrier-based Stukas it was originally hoped that a completely new design would be forthcoming. This was the Ju87T (T=Trägerflugzeug=carrier-borne), but work was stopped on this in the autumn of 1939. Instead a conversion of the standard Ju87B to suit naval requirements was taking place and the first squadron so equipped with the new aircraft, No 186, was being formed.

The Ju87C was a simple conversion, being an adaptation of the Ju87B with electrically operated outboard wing panels fitted which folded upward for stowage in the carriers' hangars. The undercarriage was made jettisonable with a view to water-borne crash-landings and an arrester hook was fitted to the rear fuselage forward of the tail-wheel which was retained. The resultant Ju87C0, and the C1 which followed, were also stressed for catapult launchings.

The few C1s delivered underwent intensive testing, but because of the limitations of range in the basic Ju87B type, it proved very unsatisfactory for naval requirements. This led to the introduction of the Ju87R as described earlier, but by this time interest in carrier-borne aircraft had lapsed and during 1941 these C1 Stukas were reconverted into standard B variants again and all further work on a navalised Stuka stopped. Later experiments with Ju88s came to nothing.

With lack of suitable aircraft, work on the carrier faltered and again came to a standstill in August 1940. All her heavy anti-aircraft weapons were stripped from her and used ashore and it was estimated that it would take a year to provide her with a new set. Also higher priorities in other fields, notably in fire-control equipment, led to further delays and although 80% complete she was towed away and laid up.

Experience of the power of ship-based aviation finally led to a reappraisal of German policy and in 1942 it was planned to com-

Below: Rudel's personal mount in the fight against the Soviet tank hordes./*Franz Selinger*

plete her to a modified design, but shortage of manpower and the knowledge that no aircraft would be available to her before 1944 brought the work finally to a halt in April 1943.

With the Russian advance in 1945, the *Graf Zeppelin* was finally scuttled in the River Oder, near Stettin. Subsequently the Soviets raised her but she foundered under tow to a Russian Baltic port because they had overladen her with loot. Thus, 10 years after she had been ordered, and still incomplete, Germany's only attempt at carrier aviation passed away.

Nor was this the only aspect of maritime warfare that the Luftwaffe neglected and it was not until 1941 that it really became interested in large-scale torpedo-bomber operations on the lines of the Regia Aeronautica Aerosiluranti units which had scored some notable successes with this weapon in the Mediterranean.

Until December 1941 all attempts by the small band of enthusiasts to obtain a suitable aerial torpedo for use with élite squadrons came to grief. Technical development was stubbornly blocked by the Navy, but some experiments with Heinkel He111 bombers was started at Grossenbrode. After a special conference at the technical office in that month, a demand was made that a special commissioner should be appointed to control torpedo development, training, supply and operations, and within the month Harlinghausen was appointed to this position.

The whole torpedo-bomber school was re-established at Grosseto, south of Leghorn, and, working closely with the Italians, trials began to find the most suitable aircraft types. Among aircraft tested was the Ju87, which was modified to carry one externally-slung torpedo, but the limited range of this aircraft ruled out any further developments. Instead the Heinkel He111 and the Junkers Ju88 were found to be the most readily adaptable, having speed and range and the capability of carrying two torpedoes. The first torpedo-bomber squadron was equipped with He111s (I/KG26), and despatched to Norway to strike at the Russian convoys. No further work was done with the Stuka in this field.

It is convenient here to follow up the remaining types and modifications of the Stuka airframe until the war's end.

It was the Russian front and, above all, the enormous numbers of the strong T-34 tanks that the Soviets were able to deploy there, which caused the majority of modifications to the Stuka and ensured its continued existence in the front line. Although its ground-support and tank-smashing rôle was well established, the slow speed of the Ju87 was proving a terrible handicap.

The defending Army was committing a large percentage of its strength to anti-aircraft weaponry and the Russians' habit of firing everything it had at German aircraft, although wasteful in the extreme, resulted over a long period in crippling losses, especially among the ground-support units.

Hauptmann Rudel had now established himself as the leading exponent of tank-smashing and enjoyed legendary fame, but in this art he was emulated by only a few, it requiring a special knack to knock out tanks with bombs or light guns, and he was still not satisfied with the MG151/20 guns which equipped the Ju87 at this time. The technical office finally came up with a 37mm cannon (Flak 18), which fired anti-tank tracer shells and developed a muzzle velocity of 2,158·9 ft/sec. A Ju87D3 was extensively modified to withstand the recoil of two of these weapons which were fitted under a reinforced wing section outboard of the undercarriage.

Tests carried out against T-34s proved conclusively that not even this sturdy, tough tank could withstand hits from the rear with such a weapon and the Ju87G1 was born. It was used to equip a tenth Panzer Staffel in StGs1, 2, 3 and 77. This additional Staffel consisted of 12 Ju87G 'Kannonenvogel' (Cannonbird) aircraft armed with the 37mm cannon, and four with bombs, these latter being used to attack anti-aircraft batteries. The cannon could be taken from the former and replaced with bomb-loads when there were no tank targets.

Thus were the above units equipped on the Eastern Front and a few went to North Africa and France. Although the cannon made the aircraft extremely unwieldy, it made the 'Kannonenvogel' an extremely potent weapon and Rudel himself knocked out over 500 Soviet tanks and thousands of thin-skinned vehicles, earning for himself a special medal designed for him by the Führer himself, and the title in the Soviet Union of 'People's Enemy Number One'!

During 1942 it had been intended to run down production of the Ju87 series and replace it with new specially designed ground-support aircraft. Two machines were competing as the Stuka's replacement, the Me210 and the Hs129. Both types failed to come up to expectations. The Me210, described by Maj Brücker, a leading exponent of ground support, as 'the most unsatisfactory aircraft Germany ever built', finally only entered service after many modifications, in 1944.

The Hs129 also failed to achieve the tasks required of it; the power units, French Gnome-Rhône engines, failed to develop the power required and proved exceedingly vulnerable to ground fire and dust, and the top speed of this aircraft turned out to be a

mere 20mph faster than the Ju87, which was already in mass production. Only one squadron of Hs129s saw service and the result of their actions was that Milch was requested to step up the output of the Ju87 in order to maintain the operational strength of the units, rather than finally kill it off.

Continuing the series, the final version of the Stuka was the Ju87H. This was a rebuilt version of the Ju87D1 with the armament removed, dual controls fitted, no dive-brakes and was used for training. The rear section of the cockpit canopy was fitted with transparent side blisters to improve the instructor's view.

In addition to basic marks the suffix letter U was given to various modifications of standard types. These were small batches, sometimes even merely 'one offs', and experimental ideas. For example, a Ju87B modified to carry an airfoil-shaped container instead of a bomb-load. Thus fitted, essential supplies could be rushed to forward areas cut off. Similarly a Ju87D had twin personnel container blisters mounted atop the wings abreast the cockpit for the transportation of ambulance patients to rear areas and for the flying out of encircled positions of stretcher cases. The Ju87B2/U4 featured ski fitments for operations in the Arctic Circle, but trials in the winter of 1941–42 proved unsatisfactory and the aircraft was reconverted.

Increased fighter opposition drove the Stukas out of the day skies during 1944–45 but some units were equipped with special engine exhaust flame-dampeners for night missions over Allied lines. The operations of these units, the Nachtschlacht Gruppen, are described in detail in Chapter 12.

A successor to the Stuka was planned by the Junkers Flugzeug und Motorenwerke but it never left the drawing board. This was the Ju187 designed at Dessau to feature a retractable landing gear, a Jumo 213 engine and a remote-control gun barbette. Tests with a model in the wind tunnel indicated that even then no great improvement was possible, 37mph being the maximum excess over the Ju87D, and with the continued development of the fighter-bomber types initiated by the Allied Hurribomber types, the project was finally dropped.

Top left: The 37mm flak cannon container and clip./*Archiv Schliephake*

Centre left: Another view of the Kannonenvogel at an experimental air base./*IWM*

Left: Junkers Ju87 No 2292 with torpedo adaptation. The Stuka was in fact, *never* actually used in combat as a torpedo bomber, despite some Allied reports to the contrary.
/*Franz Selinger*

11 The Defences Harden

After holding fast throughout the terrible winter of 1941–42 the Germans felt ready, by April 1942, to return to the offensive in Russia once again. This time, in view of the losses they had suffered, it was decided to restrict the objective to one area rather than attack all along the front. With this in mind Hitler decided that the Ukraine was the area most vital to the Soviet Union and its conquest would ensure the continuation of adequate supplies for the Reich, the Crimea would be eliminated as a possible Russian base from which to attack the Rumanian oil fields, and the conquest of the Caucasus, with its own oil regions, would very likely bring Turkey into the war on his side, or at least ensure benevolent neutrality.

Therefore during April the hard-hitting Fliegerkorps VIII was established in the Crimea area under the command of Luftflotte 4, in all, a concentration of 600 aircraft, and its first task was the elimination of the Russian garrison firmly entrenched in the fortress and naval base of Sevastopol.

The attack opened on 2 June 1942, and was intense. Ground-attack units and heavy bomber formations pounded away at the stout defence works in the usual round-the-clock manner. Some bombers flew continuously and a total of 600 sorties a day were averaged, while on the first day 700 missions were flown. In all, some 2,500 tons of high explosives was rained down on this Soviet strongpoint.

On the 4th the first infantry waves went in against the most powerful fortress in the world. Despite the massive aerial bombardment, supplemented by a barrage of 1,300 heavy guns, it took a month of bitter fighting before the last Soviet defender staggered blinking into the sunlight amidst piles of rubble. Long before then a Russian breakthrough was feared at Kursk to the north and von Richthofen's Stukas were hastily ferried into Luftflotte 4's northern zone of operations.

Continuous attacks broke up the Russian armour columns and during the first week of July the German Sixth Army went over to the offensive against Voronezh. With the Stukas leading the way the 24th Panzer Division smashed its way through the Soviet defences along the River Tim and pushed its way on to its target, but for the first time the Blitzkreig technique failed to surround the main Soviet army, which retreated intact over the Don.

Below: The dust billows in the air from a south Russian airstrip during the summer drive towards the Caucasus during 1942, as four Stukas take-off in company./*Ullstein*

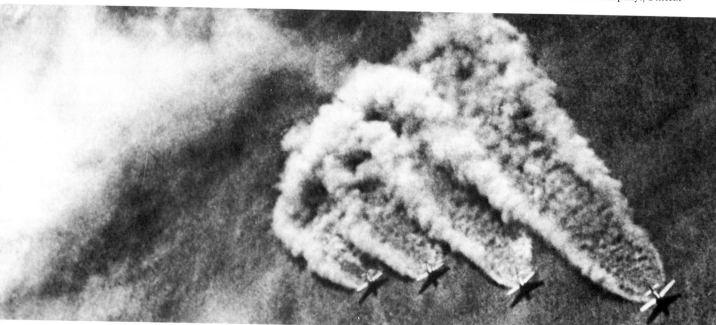

On German/Italian cooperation in the Russian zone during the summer of 1942 Friedrich Lang recalls one amusing side effect of their joint missions:

'For a short time the Italians flew Jagdschutz (fighter protection) for us in the Don bend area. As we were not satisfied with their flying they gave us an award, presenting the Ju87 Staffel-kapitänen the bronze, and the Gruppenkommandeur the silver Tapger-keitsmedaille (Medal for bravery) to sooth our feelings!'

It was at this time that the Stukas were flying close-support missions almost daily in the region of Stalingrad. II/StG2 'Immel-mann' had been joined by Dr Ernst Kupfer who, before he joined the Luftwaffe had been a captain in a cavalry regiment that was stationed in Bamberg. The 7th Staffel, which he had previously commanded, he therefore christened his 7th Schwadron (7th Squadron) to keep his links with his cavalry past. Friedrich Lang also recalls another way he kept the memory of his old unit alive: 'Dr Kupfer adopted as the II Gruppe emblem the Bamberg Reiter (Rider) which he had painted up to represent the stone sculpture of this figure in Bamberg Cathedral.'

Nevertheless the German offensive rolled southward down the Don towards the Volga. Passing Rostov through to the distant Caucasus, everywhere it seemed that nothing could this time hold back the grey hordes of the Wehrmacht. But at the loop of the Volga stood the city of Stalingrad, and here Gen Paulus and his Sixth Army became fatally bogged down trying to take the city street by street.

Fliegerkorps VIII was in the heart of this vicious battle, StG2 Stukas flying sorties

Above: During June 1942 the Stukas of Luftflotte 4 pounded the fortress of Sevastopol non-stop. Here a Gruppen is silhouetted against the dusk sky en route to the target area yet again./*Ullstein*

Right: At Sevastapol, concentrated Stuka attacks devastated these giant 30.5cm naval gun emplacements of the *Maxim-Gorki* battery guarding the city and naval base. /*Wolfinger via Archiv Schliephake*

against pin-point targets at the rate of four or more a day in a frantic attempt to crush the fanatical resistance of the defenders. For three months the battle raged as the German troops inched their way forward through the wilderness of masonry. Rudel, with the 'Immelmann' Wing, described the daily missions against the unseen enemy amid the rubble:

'On our photographic maps of the city every house is distinguishable. Each pilot is given his target precisely marked with a red arrow. We fly in, map in hand, and it is forbidden to release a bomb before we have made sure of the target and the exact position of our own troops. Flying over the western part of the city just behind the front, one is struck by the quiet prevailing there and by the almost normal traffic. Everyone, including civilians, go about their business as if the city were far behind the front. The whole western part is in our hands, only the small eastern quarter of the city towards the Volga contains these Russian nests of resistance and is the scene of our most furious assaults. Often the Russian flak dies down in the afternoon, presumably because by then they have used up the ammunition brought up across the river the night before.'*

Hitler became obsessed with the city. It was not to be by-passed, it must be taken, house by house, he decreed, and so the Sixth Army bled to death, division by division. Each was

*Hans-Ulrich Rudel; *Stuka Pilot*; Euphorion, Dublin.

Above: On the prowl. A brace of Kannonenvogel tank-busters in search of T34s./*Bundesarchiv*

Left: A group of Italian Stuka pilots pose in front of their aircraft on an Sicilian airfield. These men are of 208 Squadriglia of 101° Gruppo./*AMI via N. Malizia*

Top right: A Jumo 211J-engined Stuka./*IWM*

Centre right: Profile of the Ju87D./*IWM*

Above right: A Ju87DZ. This aircraft was fitted with the Jumo 211 engine and a wooden prop. /*Archiv Schliephake*

Right: Winter in Eastern Europe. The winter months proved one of the biggest enemies for the Luftwaffe in Russia, that of 1941/42 being one of the hardest on record, and serviceability rapidly fell among front-line units operating in primitive conditions./*Bundesarchiv*

ground down until exhausted and then replaced by another. And while the Germans fed their reserves into this Verdun in reverse, fresh Soviet armies massed on their flanks. On 19 November the Russians counterattacked. Thrusting through weak Rumanian defences to the north of the city, they poured through in a flood of Asiatic men and American machines and nothing could stop them in their great encircling movement.

The Stukas were rushed into the breakthrough areas and made sortie after sortie against the masses of T-34s, destroying scores, but with the ground forces swept away there was nothing to hold the line secured by their efforts which were all in vain. Reliance on the Stukas had become so great among the German infantry that they automatically expected them to halt any Soviet tank breakthrough. So they tended to lie down and allow the T-34s to pass over them and into their rear, knowing that the Ju87s would deal with them. With a breakthrough on such a massive scale there were not enough Stukas to plug all the gaps and the Stalingrad pocket was cut off.

This pocket became smaller and smaller and a massive airlift to keep the entrapped soldiers on their feet failed miserably with heavy losses to the Ju52 and He111 units thus employed. StG2 operated within the pocket until almost the last but finally the surviving aircraft had to be flown out and on 31 January 1943, Gen Paulus surrendered.

This disaster to German arms was the prelude; coupled with the British victory in Egypt and the landings in North Africa, it was to prove the turning point. From now on, with a few notable exceptions, the Stukas would be fighting a defensive war, retreating continually, sometimes daily, to hastily prepared air strips, often with no covering troops or flak units. Sortie rates continued at new peaks and losses through exhaustion exceeded those inflicted by the enemy.

Even so the Stukas were able to give the Soviet hordes frequent sharp lessons, such as the massacre at Morosovskaya. A strong Russian armoured column operating far in the rear of German troops threatened to overwhelm this town which the Germans had built up as a major supply base. No soldiers stood in the path of this onslaught, but by a magnificent stint of last-minute organising Oberst Kühl managed to scramble every available unit, including StG2 commanded by Maj Kupfer. On Christmas Day these aircraft caught the Russian armour out in the open steppe and inflicted massive casualties on them Added emphasis to their attack was given to the Stuka pilots on learning of the fate of their transport section, overrun by a Russian column on their airstrip at Tazinskaja. The Germans retook this field briefly in a counter-attack and found the remains of their compatriots, 'the corpses are completely mutilated, with eyes gouged out and ears and noses cut off'.

In February the retreat was halted and prevented from becoming a rout and a limited operation to retake Kursk was mounted. Oberstleutnant Weiss former Inspector of Ground Attack units, took over the Stuka and ground attack aircraft and combined them into a common strike force. The Ju87s, operating from the Stalino area, proved their worth again and on 15 March German troops re-entered Kharkov. Belograd was also taken but the offensive ground to a standstill and Kursk remained in Soviet hands.

When the front finally crystallised it left a prominent Russian salient around Kursk and during the days of April and May the Germans surrounded this outcropping section of enemy terrain with massive Panzer forces. The

Above: Junkers Ju87G2 fitted with the tank-busting cannon that gave the Stuka a new lease of life./*Archiv Schliephake*

Left: On the Eastern Front a Kette gets ready for a mission from an improvised airstrip in Russia sporting their winter colour scheme./*Bundesarchiv*

Below left: A gaggle of Ju87Ds over the Eastern Front. /*Ullstein*

Above: A Junkers Ju87R of the Luftwaffe's dwindling strength, parked at Trapani Milo airfield early in 1943./*N. Malizia*

object of the concentration was a gigantic pincer movement ,at which the Germans had become so expert, designed to cut off Kursk and trap the Soviet armies within the salient. The newly constructed tank-busting units of Schlachtgeschwader were now re-equipped and reformed under Bruno Meyer, and, operating under a re-formed Fliegerkorps VIII, were to be the key to the offensive. Once again the Stukas, with new weapons, were to assist them in their classic rôle of smashing a way through the enemy defences for the Panzer and Schlachtgeschwader to exploit. Unfortunately the idea was no longer new, the Russians had learnt all there was to know about this type of warfare after two years, and were ready to combat it, and also, once the opportunity arose, to duplicate it.

Operation Citadel was launched on 5 July and Meyer had, to carry out his mission, no less than 14 Gruppen of ground-attack aircraft, including the new Hs129s and Fw190 fighter-bombers, as well as the Ju87s. Operating from Orel was Hauptmann Lang's III/StG1 and StG1 and StG2 were operating their Stukas in both conventional rôles and mixed patrols with Kannonenvogel Flak 18 aircraft supported by others armed with 1,100lb bombs, SD2 anti-personnel bombs and machine gun packs.

The battle of Kursk was the largest tank battle in history with over a thousand armoured vehicles on either side slugging it out across the huge battle front. The Stuka units were in continuous demand for not even the superb Tigers of the German Panzer Divisions could cope with the dug-in hordes of T-34 and Stalin tanks employed by the Russian defenders.

To deal with the Stukas the Soviets had taken to concentrating a large number of mobile heavy and light flak guns on platforms in among their tank squadrons and the losses of German ground-support formations mounted accordingly. The Russians had always been great masters of camouflage and it was put to great effect during this battle. The usual system was, therefore, for the bomb-carrying Stukas to locate these mobile flak batteries and destroy them before the cannon-firing aircraft went in to eliminate the tanks themselves, but after a time the Soviet flak gunners learnt this trick and would hold their fire until the aircraft were committed, and thus the point and counter-point raged.

It was no sinecure either for the slow Stukas to find themselves caught between opposing lines of tanks and artillery. The air space between the lines became filled with shells from the two duellists and it became common for units to lose aircraft in this manner when sandwiched in this way. Life expectancy in the Stuka Gruppen dropped rapidly over Kursk but there was no denying their effectiveness.

It soon became clear that in the Kursk offensive the Germans had bitten off more than they could chew, and despite enormous losses they failed to penetrate the Soviet defences. Worse, the Russians felt strong enough to counter-attack on the Orel front and again the Stukas had to be rapidly switched from one side of the salient to the other to plug holes in the defences. By the end of July the Panzers, smashed and broken, had been forced back beyond their start lines. The last great German offensive on the Eastern Front had failed.

Nor was it only in Eastern Europe that the defences against the Stukas were getting the upper hand. At sea also considerable rearmament of warships and merchantmen had fast led to a situation where to attack any sort of large naval squadron or strongly defended convoy was a prickly job for an airman. The belated introduction of the 20mm Oerlikon gun had already provided all warships from battleship down with a strong field of fire, but more important was the fitting during 1943 of large numbers of the Bofors 40mm gun, in single, twin and quadruple mountings. This weapon fired a large enough shell to break up an attacking plane in mid-air, and could provide a daunting barrage in the face of torpedo- or dive-bombing.

With an end of the Tunisian Campaign most of the Stukas in the Mediterranean under German control were withdrawn to the Balkans well away from Allied fighters, although the Italians still continued to use them in small quantities without much effect. When the Allies invaded Sicily in July 1943 most of the forward airfields had already been rendered useless by a combination of continuous bombing and heavy rain. The only Stuka success of the entire operation was the sinking of the American destroyer *Maddow*.

But it was in the Aegean campaign which followed the invasion of Italy, that the Stuka dive-bomber reasserted itself, for the final time, as a warship-buster. For in late 1943 it seemed that the clock had been put back two years and that the battle of Crete was being fought all over again, regardless of the bitter lesson learnt there.

The battle for Crete had shocked the world, proving the power of the dive-bomber, but since then the lesson had surely been absorbed and digested. Heavy anti-aircraft fire-power aboard warships was now accepted and most ships were now liberally equipped with some form of defence. The real key to the defeat of the dive-bomber had, as long ago as August 1940, been shown to be strong fighter cover. In 1941 it had still not existed but in the Mediterranean battleground of 1943 surely the Allies had the strength and more to spare to prevent any such repetition, it seemed unthinkable that it should be otherwise.

The majority of Allied observers seemed to agree that the threat of the Stuka was past, it was an obsolete weapon when faced by organised and determined defences, and modern equipment. Fear was a thing of the past. Sir Frederick Pile, head of the British AA defences wrote: 'As a matter of fact, the effect of the dive-bomber was largely a moral one and could be trained against. In AA Command we had a dive-bombing school where all our light AA gunners were sent, with the result that they gained sufficient confidence to stand up to any dive-bomber in the world.'*

*Gen Sir Frederick Pile; *Ack-Ack*; Harrap, London.

In addition to enhanced AA protection, the Allies had thousands of aircraft operating in the Central Mediterranean area by the autumn of 1943; by contrast the Germans' total strength by that time amounted to around 1,200 aircraft only, of all types.

When Italy surrendered in September, the Allied high command had hoped to take advantage of this and seize the important island of Rhodes, long recognised as the key to the Aegean Sea. Detailed planning went on resulting in Operation Accolade, but preparations for the mounting of this invasion were postponed by the Salerno and Anzio operations and finally the landings in the south of France. Instead a scaled-down operation, relying on speed and the confused position prevailing in September, was proposed, which by some of the lesser islands of the Aegean would be seized and held.

The benefits of control of the Aegean were great, for besides pointing a dagger at the heart of the Balkans, which the Russians were soon to threaten from the north-east, the successful clearing of Axis forces from this area might prove instrumental in bringing Turkey into the war on the Allied side, or so they reasoned.

Initially all went well and several islands, Casteloriso, Cos, Leros, Samos and Stampalia, were occupied by raiding force groups. But if the Allies were interested in securing the Aegean, then Hitler was equally determined to hold on to his foothold there. He had always held that these island bases were essential and to prove his belief he reacted swiftly and vigorously to the Allied move.

Above: Stuka pilot catches up with his mail on the Eastern Front. Note the starter motor on wheels and the arctic clothing. */Wolfinger via Archiv Schliephake*

Left: Perfect bombing. In the vast hinterland of the Soviet Union the precision bombing of the Stuka was directed at vital river crossings with consistent success./*Lehmann*

Below: Bleak surroundings for this lonely Stuka./*Hans Obert*

Bottom: On-the-spot check-out for a 'Dora'./*Hans Obert*

Before the Italian surrender on 8 September and 3 October the Luftwaffe rushed in reinforcements from every major front and over 100 aircraft reinforced the south-east sector during that period. Ju88 units were flown in from France, Bf109s from Austria and the Stuka units moved in from Russia. StG3 and StG151 were in position by early September and soon commenced operations; StG3 being based initially in Greece but soon moved to Rhodes, while StG151 operated from Croatia.

Thus, in a series of swift moves, the Germans established local air superiority over the whole combat area. The Aegean islands were beyond the range of all but a few long-range fighters of the Middle East Air Force, and although 201 Naval Co-Operation squadron acted with vigour at every opportunity, they could not effectively sway the issue. Six squadrons of long-range Lightnings were loaned for a brief period during October by General Eisenhower but after their withdrawal the troops and warships supplying them were on their own.

The Germans soon made it clear that they meant to fight for the islands and on 21 September the Stukas were heavily in action securing the flanks of Greece. They supported the suppression of the island of Cephallonia at the mouth of the Gulf of Corinth and followed this up by smashing artillery and defence works on Corfu on the 24th. Next day they were pounding Split off the Yugoslavian coast, quickly eliminating opposition and enabling a rapid occupation by follow-up troops. It was clear by the speed and effectiveness of these attacks that in one respect the Stukas had lost none of their old skills. It should have acted as a warning to the defenders of Leros but it was decided to try and hold these islands despite the risk.

Their flanks secure, the Stuka formations were rapidly transferred to the main operational area. Supplies were being rushed into the islands by British destroyer flotillas and they also used their time returning from these missions to hunt and destroy Axis convoys bringing up reinforcements. They had already scored several outstanding victories in the area, but the pointer to the future was clearly made when a force of Ju88s caught the destroyer *Intrepid* and the Greek *Queen Olga* in Leros harbour on the 26th and sank them both.

Rhodes was wrested from the numerically superior Italian garrison on 12 September and the whole strength of StG3 quickly moved in accompanied by a Bf109 force. This meant that the whole of the Aegean Sea was within their range. Surface striking forces continued to move in despite this and a British force, which included the destroyer *Eclipse*, succeeded in sinking a 2,500 ton freighter off Rhodes on the 23rd. The escorting German destroyer, TA10 was hit and driven ashore.

By the beginning of October the Germans were in a position to launch the first of their brilliant offensives and on the 3rd and 4th of the month they assaulted Cos. Out of 300 sorties flown by the Luftwaffe in support of this occupation over half were flown by the Ju87s. British troops offered stubborn resistance in the face of this attack but the Italian garrison put up no fight and the island was quickly taken.

It became abundantly clear that Leros was the next on the German list and a frantic endeavour was made to build up the British garrison there in order to forestall this. Braving the sky now completely dominated by the Luftwaffe, small ships of the Royal Navy Levant Command, destroyers, MTBs, caiques and motor launches, daily ventured into the besieged island with troops and supplies. To further forestall the German build-up the destroyer patrols were reinforced by the addition of six cruisers with good AA batteries and further reinforcements of Hunt class destroyers. The stage was thus set for the last of the classic duels between warship and Stuka. By all accounts the scales should now have shifted in favour of the Navy: the Stuka was to show otherwise.

On the night of 6/7 October a British force consisting of the light cruisers *Sirius* and *Penelope*, escorted by the destroyers *Faulknor* and *Fury*, scored an impressive victory by intercepting and destroying a complete convoy bound for Rhodes – with specialist personnel. In all, an ammunition ship, an armed trawler

118

Above left: A 'Dora' on a snowswept forward airstrip. /*Hans Obert*

Left: Dr Ernst Kupfer and his mount, featuring the *Bamberg Reiter* on its nose./*Hans Obert*

Above: Wrapped up against the elements are the Stukas of 3/StG2./*Hans Obert*

and six F-lighters were sunk. The British squadron then stood southward towards daybreak but they had left their withdrawal too late.

At first light the dive-bombers of StG3, aided by Ju88s and escorted by Bf109s, were airborne and located the warships steaming south through the Scarpanto Strait. The attacks continued for as long as the ships were in range and a brief appearance by two American Lightnings only provided a slight respite. The Stukas managed to plant a 1,100lb bomb into the *Penelope*, which so damaged her that her speed was reduced to 23kts, but the ship was saved by the fact that the bomb failed to explode.

Nothing daunted, the Royal Navy resumed the patrols the following night but this time a strong umbrella of Lightnings was arranged for dawn. Thus it was when the Stukas found the ships at midday on 9 October, they had to attack through this strong aerial defence. StG3 suffered heavily, the Lightning claiming 15 and the warships' guns three, but their losses, although only half as many as claimed, were unable to prevent them scoring devastating hits on several warships.

The cruiser *Carlisle* (3,500 ton) took a heavy bomb aft and came to a halt, immobilised. The destroyer *Panther* (1,540 ton) also received a direct hit and sank immediately. Strenuous afforts were made to save the *Carlisle* and eventually she was got under tow by the *Rockwood*. Although she finally reached Alexandria her damage was so extensive that she was never repaired.

Throughout the rest of the month after the American long-range fighters had been withdrawn, the warships played a wary game of cat and mouse with the Luftwaffe, patrolling by night and withdrawing to neutral Turkish waters or laying up in remote harbours by day. Even so losses were severe. The dive-bombers hit the cruiser *Sirius* on the 17th, two motor launches, Ml563 and Ml835, were sunk in Leros harbour on the 12th.

On the 24th the German bombers scored a notable success by sinking the supply ship *Taganrog* at Samos and four days later they caught the big landing craft LCT115 carrying guns and troops some 35 miles from Castelrosso and sank her. On the last day of the month the cruiser *Aurora* and the destroyer *Belvoir* were both caught out in the open, hit and damaged.

Not only the warships were subjected to non-stop bombing. Gun positions, troop emplacements and ammunition dumps were also given repeated poundings by the Ju87 and Ju88 units which mounted an average of 60 sorties a day against Leros. On November 12th the build-up in sortie ratios began with the opening of the final assault on the island. Artillery and AA positions were blasted during the following five days with missions by all types Ju87 Ju88 Bf109 Bf110 and Mc202 aircraft taking part. Although resistance was strong a paratroop drop of 500 men from Ju52s on the night of the 13th tipped the scales.

By this time the destroyers attempting to act in support of the troops ashore had even more to contend with for II/KG100 had arrived in Greece during the month and within a few days their glider bombs had disposed of the destroyers *Rockwood* and *Dulverton*.

With the fall of Leros the Allies accepted defeat and the lesser garrisons of Samos and Syros were evacuated and by the end of November the Aegean was firmly in German hands. It was the Stuka's last victory.

12 Duel in the Darkness

The failure in front of Kursk led to far-reaching changes in the structure of the Schlachtflieger which for the first time was organised as an independent arm of the Luftwaffe. With the suicide of Jeschonnek new ideas were introduced and among them was the appointment of Oberst Kupfer as the first General der Schlachtflieger, whose functions were to coordinate all ground attack units including the Stukas. Such a reform had long been overdue and was treated with enthusiasm by the crews on the spot. However Kupfer's early death in a flying accident in the Balkans in November 1943 was followed by the appointment to the new post of an old Stuka men, Waffengeneral Hitschold, who took over in December. However, his brief was for inspection, and liaison with other arms, etc, but not for operations.

Under his direction the phasing out of Ju87 and its replacement with the Fw190 was speeded up. Enough Fw190s were on hand to re-equip the SG units at the rate of about two Gruppen per six-week period and by the autumn of 1944 there was only a single Stuka Gruppe flying by day, namely Rudel's

III/StG2, but even this unit had to partially re-equip with Bückers biplanes for night operations at the beginning of 1945, as the production of Ju87s had been finally stopped in October 1944.

Meanwhile during 1943–44 things went from bad to worse on the Russian Front for the Luftwaffe. Kharkov fell to the Red Army on 23 August, Kiev on 6 November, although shortly after this a local victory achieved by the German Army with Stuka support helped to stabilise the front for a brief spell. But even this short respite was only achieved at heavy cost, 'Immelmann' Gruppe, for example, losing Hauptmanns Herling, Fritsch and Krumings, all holders of the Iron Cross for their ground-attack work, in just one week over this sector.

Heavy rainfall throughout the battle reduced most of the Stuka airstrips to quagmires in which the bombers became ensnared. In order to overcome this the wheel spats were often jettisoned to allow free rotation, and so prevalent did this problem become that serious study was made of a modification to the undercarriage. Thus the Ju87D5 incorporated a

Below: Ground shot of the Kannonenvogel, note the kills registered on her nose./*IWM*

120

jettisonable undercarriage for emergency field operations and the Ju87F was an experimental type which featured oversize tyres in a further attempt to overcome this difficulty, but this version never attained production status.

Meanwhile the Soviets had built up their forces and renewed their offensive west of Kiev. This in turn meant that all close-support aircraft had yet again to be hurriedly redeployed from the lower Dnieper region. The renewed and heavy pressure, made worse by the atrocious weather conditions, resulted in the falling back of the Germans all along the line. Soon the Russians began to threaten Rumania and the Crimea was abandoned. All along the Eastern and Italian fronts 1944 saw the Germans retreating, and it was also apparent that the Allied invasion of France would not be long delayed either, which would place Germany in an unenviable position.

Although production of aircraft was not greatly hampered, and indeed increased all through the year, the shortage of fuel was playing an increasing part in reducing the effectiveness of the Luftwaffe to dispute control of the sky. Hitschold later commented that this was the overall decisive factor and first became noticeable to him when he was Kommandeur of Stuka Schule I at Werthem between November 1941 and June 1942. He was forced to slow down training, even at that time, so that a two-month course took over five months to complete. After Stalingrad then, and later, it was this strangulation of fuel supply which led to the failure of the SG units to stop the Russian offensives in January. But although the autumn of 1944 saw the end of the Stuka in the daylight skies over Europe, the aircraft itself was to find

Top: Defensive armament improved as fighter opposition grew. This is the MG81Z machine gun.
/*Archiv Schliephake*

Above: The Dobbas transportation pack.
/*Archiv Schliephake*

Right: The wing-mounted 7.9mm MG17 gun.
/*Archiv Schliephake*

a full and useful rôle as a night attack bomber.

The idea of the Nachtschlacht Gruppen is said to have arisen from the success which the Russians, suffering under air superiority, had with the U-2 light aircraft of the spotter type, in nuisance bombing operations over the front areas at night, early in the war. The Luftwaffe had followed suit in the autumn of 1942, employing Arado Ar66, Gotha Go145 and even Fieseler Storch types, which they formed into Störkampf Staffeln. It was not until late in 1943, however, that the first actual NSG came into being.

At that time Richthofen, then in command of Luftflotte 2 was trying the Italian Cr42 biplane as a night attack aircraft. In January, when the Nettuno landing took place, he asked for a Staffel of Ju87s, about the usefulness of which Hitschold was rather sceptical on account of the predominance of Allied night-fighters. However, the success of that Staffel led to the formation of NSG9 and to further employment of the NSGs in the west.

During 1944 the creation of further NSGs went on apace, the crews being drawn from existing Störkampf Staffeln as well as Fw190 pilots who proved unsuitable for the SGs, also pilots from disbanded bomber units and ex-instructors. Unit commanders were largely drawn from bomber units. Most of the aircraft came from the SGs which had been converted to Fw190s and there proved enough Ju87s to form NSG 1, 2, 4, 8 and 9; NSG 3 and 5 were equipped with Ar66 and Gotha Go145 while NSG 7 was given Cr42s. NSG units had an established strength of 60 aircraft, three Staffeln of 20 each.

Meanwhile the Russian bulldozer had continued to roll forward but it was not until

10 June, with the Allies firmly ashore in Normandy, that the Soviets permitted themselves the launching of their main offensive in the east. The initial thrust was against the Finns and a Gruppen of Stukas had to be hurriedly rushed from the Narva front to the assistance of their allies. The offensive of the central front opened on 23 June and it proved impossible for the Germans to hold it; by 3 July Minsk had fallen.

Throughout July the bulk of the SGs with their steadily reducing numbers of Stukas, were thrown into the cauldron, leaving no reserves, but the Russian advance into Poland continued despite fierce resistance, and Brest-Litovsk, target of the intiial German attack in the far-off days of 1941, fell on the 28th. To the south the Russian attack carried the defence line of the River Pruth and the Rumanians cracked and fell back. Following the coup which overthrew their Government further reinforcements, including 40 Ju87s were transferred to Rumania from Estonia. StG2 had two of its Gruppen transferred south to Buzau north of Bucharest.

Flying around the clock against the endless columns of tanks and vehicles it soon became apparent that the retreat had become a rout and wholesale desertion by Rumanian units led to many German holding troops being cut off and surrounded. Rudel's unit, III/StG2, had the unique experience towards the last days of August of operating against Soviet tanks from an airfield surrounded by Rumanian troops and flak units which were then on the opposing side. By this time Constanza had fallen and then the oilfields at Ploesti went. With the capture of Bucharest on the 31st all Luftwaffe units were hastily evacuated

Below: A Ju87 of the Nachtschlacht units undergoing maintenance. Their nocturnal operations taken at high risk and great intensity, marked the swan-song of the Stuka in Western Europe. */Ullstein*

over to Hungary and Bulgaria. This latter nation, faced with the prospect of bitter fighting on its own soil, hastily changed sides at the approach of Russian armour, necessitating another hasty move for the Germans.

In the north, Finland likewise threw in the towel but by sheer hard fighting some semblance of a front was maintained. As the autumn passed the Germans abandoned position after position and there was little the depleted ranks of the Stukas could do to help. The remaining SG units were thrown into a vain attempt to hold the Soviet advance on Budapest but by the end of the year this city had also fallen.

Comparative strengths of the Eastern Front and the forces available to defeat an invasion of France in June 1944 show just how much the western area had been run down. In Ground Attack strength the figures were France 75, Italy 50, Eastern Front 550. The bulk of the aircraft in France and Italy were of the Nachtschlacht Gruppen.

Although it is the considered opinion of senior German officers that the Nachtschlacht units came too late, because the crews were insufficiently trained and effective day reconnaissance was badly lacking, this development was clearly the only way in which the Stukas in the west could operate. As a specialist type of operation carried out with some success by an aircraft declared obsolete as early as 1941, the Nachtschlacht deserves detailed description as the final rôle of the Ju87.

NSG1, after operating on the Russian Front with Arado Ar66s and Gotha Go145s, had its crews withdrawn to Kaunas in April 1944 for conversion to Ju87s. In May the first Staffel moved to Stubendorf, while the 2nd and 3rd Staffeln went to Gross Stein for Blind Flying training with SG111, which in December 1943 had superseded Blindflug Schule 11 at the latter airfield. SG111 under the command of Maj Kraus, was the night flying training school of all subsequent NSG units.

Early in June NSG1 transferred to Wormditt, where four new crews were collected, and some three days later it moved to Grieslienen for formation, flying and bombing practice. Towards the end of June the Gruppe returned to operations on the Latvian front and about three months later, in September, was withdrawn to Wormditt, where the Ju87s were equipped with the FuGe 25A and FuGe 16Z,* and W/T operators were given instruction in the use of the latter.

On 20 October 1944, aircraft and crews of the three Staffeln moved from Wormditt to Bönninghardt/South in preparation for commencing operations on the Western Front; the Gruppe assembled at that airfield towards the end of that month. Meanwhile NSG2 had its 1st and 3rd Staffeln based at Wahn, NSG3 and 4 were operating in Hungary and NSG5 in Italy.

By the beginning of November the operational strength of NSG1 was 15 aircraft in three Staffeln. The fixed establishment strength was 15 aircraft and crews per Staffel and the difference between this and the operational strength was largely accounted for by the fact that a number of aircraft and crews had remained behind at Wormditt, whilst others had remained at Störmede,

*FuGe = Funk Gerat (Radio set).

Below: 'Doras' lined up ready for their next assignment. /*Hans Obert*

123

where they had made an intermediate stop in transferring from East Prussia to Bönninghardt/South. In addition, three crews had been detached to NSG2 soon after arrival.

All aircraft of the Gruppe were Ju87D5s, equipped with the FuGe25A, and it was intended to use this in conjunction with the Egon procedure.* The majority of the aircrew had considerable operational experience gained on the Eastern and Mediterranean fronts and most of the pilots had come from dissolved Stuka units; they consisted mainly of men found unfit for retraining as fighter pilots. Both the 1st and 3rd Staffeln of NSG2 at Wahn were up to establishment strength of 15 aircraft each. These units were equipped with Ju87D5s specially fitted out for the task in hand.

For pilot protection there was fitted, in addition to the usual bullet-resisting glass screen of about 4cm thickness, armour plating

Right: The *Bamberg Reiter* of II/StG2./Hans Obert

Below: Brief respite for a 2/StG2 crew./Hans Obert

Bottom: Celebration drink and garland on the Eastern front. /Hans Obert

*The Egon procedure was a method of ground controlling bombers by radio. A mobile transmitting unit was attached to the NSG formations operating in Western Europe.

of 10mm thickness. This was fitted to ensure seat and leg protection against fire from below, and back, shoulders and head protection against fire from astern. The wireless operator was similarly protected with seat and leg protection against fire from below, two adjustable shields attached to guns for hand protection, and side plates up to knee height to give lateral protection. All repairs for the NSG units on the Western Front were carried out at Köln/Ostheim airfield.

The following tactics were employed by the NSG units, against targets which included, in their order of priority, troops preparing to attack, artillery positions, tanks and M/T concentrations and M/T supply routes. Crews were invariably given a definite objective and no free-lance operations were flown nor were ground-strafing attacks carried out.

On occasion an alternative target was given at the briefing and the crews were sometimes told that if they were unable to locate or attack the given target, they were to release their bombs over any suitable concentration of ground forces observed.

Bombloads included HE, fragmentation and incendiary types, according to the nature of the target assigned. On rare occasions bomb loads as heavy as 1,500lb or even 1,800lb were taken.

Close contact was maintained between the NSG unit and the 'Flivo' (GAF liaison officer) attached to the German ground forces, and operations were often laid on at short notice as a result of requests received through that officer. Prior to an operation, advance notice was sent to Flak units and ground forces in the area over which the flight was to be made. The standard laid down with regard to weather conditions was that a minimum of 4/10ths cloud was required for cover purposes, and visibility of at least 3km was necessary. Operations were not flown during the period extending from about three days before to three days after a full moon.

During the briefing, careful instruction was given on the location of the German front line positions, even to the extent of cross-questioning members of the crews to make sure they had understood the position. Here can be seen a faint tremor of the Führer's concern for his infantry units, who he knew to be having a very rough war, while he considered the Luftwaffe crews to be having an extremely soft one.

The Ju87s took off individually at fixed intervals which varied from one to five minutes, and flew independently to their objective. After flying at about 1,000ft, they would commence to climb when approaching the Allied front so as to attain a height of from 3,500 to 7,000ft when crossing the lines; altitudes between these two limits were considered best for bombing, so that an effective spread of anti-personnel bombs was ensured. After the release of the bombs, height was lost to between 600 and 1,000ft and the homeward course was flown at about this altitude. The speeds flown by the Stukas on operations were as follows:

Outward flight at heights of about 1,000ft – 250–260km/h.
Outward flight after climbing to the usual operational altitude – 260–270km/h.
Homeward flight at low altitude – about 270 km/h.

Navigation was solely by DR with the help of navigational aids such as visual beacons, marker searchlights, and Flak tracer fired in the direction of flight, and flares were often used to mark the target. These marker flares were laid by certain of the NSG aircraft flying on the operation, and were usually carried by the first and third aircraft flying on the operation, and were usually of the normal parachute flare type which were released from 2,500 to 3,000ft.

Two colours were employed, white or orange. The principle of flying on a given bearing for a fixed time from a datum point was likewise employed by the flare droppers; the aircraft were not equipped with electric altimeters.

The Inspector of the NSG units on the Western Front was Maj von Mopösch. Gruppenkommandeurs of NSG1 and 2 were Haupt Wilberg and Maj Müller, and both units operated with considerable success and comparative invulnerability. The very lack of

speed of the Ju87 made it an extremely difficult target for the Allied night fighters and losses to AA fire at night proved to be small.

Their biggest danger lay in the more skilled night-fighter pilots and the Mosquito squadrons operating over the front in particular notched up some high scores against the night intruder Stukas. A Mosquito from No 219 Squadron, for example, shot down three Ju87s in one night in the Nijmegen area on 2 October.

Even so this method of operating was far less costly than daylight raids in airspace now totally dominated by Allied fighters, and, operating with good results during periods of no moonlight, and later reinforced by Fw190s carrying 2,000lb bombs, the ubiquitous Stuka entered its final chapter.

A typical mission by a NSG Stuka was that carried out by Unteroffizier Kurt Griese, with Unteroffizier Walter Hein flying wireless operator/rear gunner, in a Ju87D5 against targets in the Eindhoven area on the night of 29/30 October 1944.

Some 12 or 13 Stukas, representing the total available strength of 1, 2 and 3/NSG1 were detailed for this operation, and crews were briefed to attack Allied ground forces reported to be in the wooded area in the vicinity of Weert, 25 miles south-east of Eindhoven; the target was to be marked by orange flares with an additional guide in the form of AA tracer fired on a bearing to the target in the direction of approach of the aircraft.

The crews were instructed to take-off at short intervals beginning at 0330hrs, and to

Above: Epilogue-a laden 'Dora' heads into the overcast. */Hans Obert*

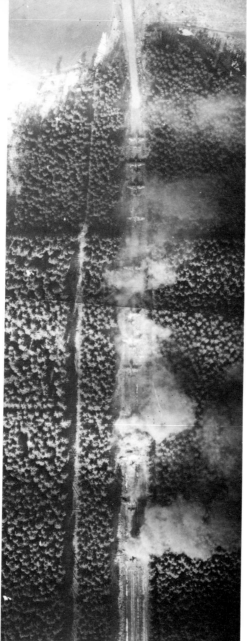

Right: All lined up to attack the Remagen bridge during the Allied advance in Europe. These Stukas were spotted at Lippe airfield and attacked by USAAF Lightnings./*USAAF*

fly independently on a course of 270° until they sighted the marker flares. This operation was the second of two almost identical sorties flown during the night of 29/30 October, the first having been made by the same crews with take-off beginning at 1800hrs.

The Stuka, carrying one 250kg container and four 50kg containers of 1kg anti-personnel bombs, took off from Bönninghardt/South airfield and flew on a due westerly course at 3,500ft. The Flak tracer and the target marker flares were duly sighted and the bombs were released over the objective.

Griese then turned his machine for home, but when still in the turn he found that the compass had become u/s and he was forced to fly blind in an attempt to regain German territory. Eventually the petrol supply ran out and he made a crash landing at a point some 20 miles east of Eindhoven. Both members of the crew were captured by British troops.

Night intruder Stukas regarded two sorties nightly as routine and in times of dire urgency

as many as five sorties were recorded in a single night! The strain was immense but the 70 old dive-bombers had to perform as if they were 700 against the overwhelming weight of the British and American forces, and even then they would have been too few.

As the Allies pushed closer to the German homeland from both east and west, the airspace in which the ever shrinking numbers of Stukas had to operate became scarcer. By now formations were fighting piecemeal on both fronts, as and when pilots and aircraft became available, but they kept fighting.

Stukas of the NSG were active during the Allied push on Aachen and in the fortnight preceding its fall flew an average of 50 sorties a night, running the gauntlet of strong Mosquito forces. With the offensive from the south by the American Third Army those Ju87s still operational, about 40 strong, were switched to that front. The desperate gamble of the Ardennes offensive and the great attack of January 1st only further depleted the ranks of the SG units and achieved nothing.

A similar offensive in Hungary produced the same result. There were still some 600 ground support aircraft available in this area, about a third of which were Ju87s, but the loss rate was climbing and the Soviet Air Force dominated the Eastern battlefields as did the RAF and USAAF the West.

Before the final collapse about 100 Stukas were scraped together to dispute the crossing of the Rhine and 50 of these operated with the NSG in the Oppenheim area on the night of 23/24 March. Lack of fuel soon cut even this meagre total by half and by April all the survivors were in the south of Germany.

When the surrender came on 8 May, large numbers of flyable and damaged Stukas were found abandoned around Munich by the advancing Americans, but Rudel defiantly flew his battered 'Immelmann' unit out of Soviet territory intact and surrendered to the Americans at Kitzingen as an undefeated Gruppe. It was a last defiant gesture.

Thus ended the Stuka story. Feared and hated by its opponents in its hey-day and derided after the Battle of Britain, the Ju87 nevertheless imprinted its inverted gull-winged shape on the history of World War II. Often called a 'Terror Weapon' by Allied propaganda during the war, no doubt as part of the effort to debunk the fear it prompted by its success, this epitaph persists to this day.

The greatest Stuka pilot of all, Hans-Ulrich Rudel, paid the following tribute to the Ju87 and its crews:
'Countless German soldiers and refugees from the Eastern Front owe their lives and freedom to the Stuka flyers.

'The missions of the German dive-bomber units were widespread and losses were high, but despite all this they were ready to fly at any time. With every alert we Stuka flyers fought very close with the troops on the ground as they had to carry the main burden of the fighting. The name "Infantry of the Air" given to us by the soldiers was a recognition that we helped our comrades on the ground and sometimes saved them from impossible situations and terrible fates.

'The story of the unique successes of Stuka pilots and gunners all over Europe and North Africa, despite their small numbers and the inferiority of their machines, is also respected by our former enemies. Even during the war the word "Stuka" meant bravery and readiness. In no other air force and in no other German flying unit were the achievements of single aircrews and squadrons even nearly as high as with the Stuka fliers.

'Finally, we must not forget that without our technical ground personnel all this would have been impossible.'

Conqueror of Continents, or Helpless Prey. Whatever the final verdict on the Stuka it will remain as one of the outstanding bomber aircraft of the period. To compare it with other types is difficult for it was unique. Only the Douglas Dauntless achieved equal status in the dive-bombing field. Another famous test pilot, Capt E. M. Brown, Royal Navy, flew all types of dive-bombers during the war, and he gave the author this assessment of how Allied dive-bomber types compared to the Stuka itself:

'True dive-bombers like the Ju87, the Dauntless and the Vengeance were of course always superior in that role to fighters, bombers or torpedo-bombers adapted for dive-bombing as a secondary role, although none of the dive-bombers I ever flew were outstanding overall performers and all needed fighter cover to operate effectively.

'The Dauntless was painfully slow and had very slow-opening dive-brakes which were a tactical disadvantage, but was rock steady in the dive although it was not easy to adjust aim in the dive because the aileron controls got very heavy as speed increased.

'The Helldiver suffered from heavy buffet in a braked dive so was most unpleasant to fly and difficult to aim on this account. The pull-out was always a hairy business because of the buffet and the dive-brakes blanking the elevator. The fact that the Helldiver was in trouble can be gauged from the fact that from the date of the first production aircraft flight in June 1942 until it went into action for the first time in November 1943, over 880 major changes in design were made.

'The Vultee Vengeance I was a poor aircraft which by major modification to become the Vengeance IV, eradicated all the original faults, until it was probably the nearest in efficiency to the Ju87.'

But if forced to judge its merits as a weapon of war, I would equate the Stuka with a surgeon's knife, deftly picking out the important target amidst a mass of irrelevant objects. By the same yardstick the four-engined bomber of the Allied Air Forces were the true Terror Weapons; sledgehammers which pulped acres of cities and people with their carpets of bombs to achieve the same result. Who shall say which weapon of the two was superior?

Left: Hans-Ulrich Rudel – the greatest Stuka pilot of them all. /*Rudel*

Below: War's end. A stripped down and forlorn abandoned Stuka in lonely isolation on a German airfield, 8 April 1945. /*IWM*

Appendices

1 Technical Data

	Ju87A	*Ju87B*	*Ju87R*	*Ju87D*
Engine:	Jumo 210C	Jumo 221Da	Jumo 221Da	Jumo 211J
Hp:	640	1,210	1,210	1,300
Wingspan	13.8m	13.8m	13.8m	13.8m
Length:	10.8m	11.1m	11.1m	11.13m
Height:	4.16m	4.24m	4.24m	4.24m
Wing area:	31.9sq m	32sq m	32sq m	32sq m
Weight Empty:	2,570kg	2,760kg	2,760kg	3,550kg
Weight full:	3,400kg	4,250kg		5,835kg
Max speed:	320km/h	380km/h	380km/h	380km/h
Cruising:	290km/h	340km/h	340km/h	340km/h
Landing speed:	108km/h	110km/h	110km/h	110km/h
Climb rate 1,000m	3.1min	2min	2min	2min
Climb rate 3,000m	23min	12min	X	X
Ceiling:	7,000m	8,100m	8,100m	6,000m
Range:	500km	800km	1,920km	1,000km

2 Luftwaffe Units

1 Luftflotte

1–6. Were organised to cover specific areas of combat and had no fixed strength, could vary from between about 200 and 1,500 aircraft.

2 Fliegerkorps

I–X. Operated within a Luftflotte or as an independent unit (eg Fliegerkorps X). Comprised all types and strength could vary between 150 and 800 aircraft.

3 Geschwader

Largest formation with fixed strength, nominally 90 aircraft in three Gruppen plus a Stab (staff) flight. Stukageschwader I indicated as StG1.

4 Gruppe

Normal strength was 27 aircraft in three Staffeln plus a Stab. 2nd Gruppe of Stukageschwader I indicated as II/StG1.

5 Staffel

Nominal strength nine aircraft. Three Staffeln to a Gruppe but later a fourth Staffel of tank-busters was added in Russia.